BURNLEY'S
GOALKEEPERS
THROUGH THE AGES

BURNLEY'S
GOALKEEPERS
THROUGH THE AGES

MIKE PROSSER

ILLUSTRATIONS BY RON BROWN

PHOTOGRAPHS BY KIND PERMISSION
OF BURNLEY FOOTBALL CLUB

DB
PUBLISHING

This book is dedicated to my late son
Marc Prosser
who died in 2009 from Cystic Fibrosis at the age of twenty-nine

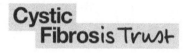

Logo © Cystic Fibrosis Trust 2017. Registered as a charity in England and Wales (1079049) and in Scotland (SC040196). A company limited by guarantee, registered in England and Wales number 3880213. Registered office: Cystic Fibrosis Trust, 2nd Floor, One Aldgate, London EC3N 1RE.

First Publishied in Great Britain in 2017 by DB Publishing,
an imprint of JMD Media Ltd

ISBN 978-1-78091-539-5

Printed and bound in the UK

CONTENTS

The world of the goalkeeper is in the spotlight for the full 90 minutes of any game. Whereas one slip from an outfield player might not be costly, one mistake from the goalkeeper and fingers point and heads shake. One serious mistake can cost the game.

If an outfield player can hide or have a quiet spell during a game, there is no such luxury for the 'keeper.

A centre forward misses a golden opportunity and a week later, if he scores, the mistake is forgotten. However, it is not so with a goalkeeper, whose mistakes can be remembered for weeks. Only the strong survive.

DAVE THOMAS 2010

FOREWORD BY TOM HEATON

I am very proud & honoured to be asked to write the foreword for this book. The book is a great example, to me, of what Burnley Football club is all about. Steeped in rich history & tradition everyone associated with the club feels that pride & passion of being a claret. That can be felt in this book. Growing up, my late Grandfather had a special place in his heart for the Clarets. Since I signed for the club in the summer of 2013, it has become very clear to me why it was so special to him & so many others.

The club has been very fortunate to have had so many top goalkeepers through time. People often talk to me about the previous goalkeepers. Alan Stevenson, Marlon Beresford & Brian 'Beast' Jensen are regularly mentioned. Alan & Marlon were a little before my time, but I can sense the pride when people talk about all of them. From Will smith, Rob Kay & William Cox in the First season of the football league all the way through to present day, I was fascinated by the names,

dates & statistics. None more so than Colin Mcdonald & Adam Blacklaw, both of whom were in the era of when my Dad started watching the clarets, as you might imagine, I heard a lot about them! All the names through the book are a great reminder that each individual is a temporary custodian of the gloves, but each has the opportunity of playing for this great club.

On a personal note, prior to arriving at Burnley FC, I always felt I was building a career, waiting for the right platform to perform on. I couldn't have found a better home than Burnley Football Club & it has felt right since the moment I walked through the door. I am very thankful, to all clarets, the Club itself, Sean Dyche & the Goalkeeping Coach Billy Mercer for that. My ambition has always been to try & emulate these Burnley Goalkeeping Heroes, working hard day in, day out & somehow try to keep the ball out of the net!

I hope you enjoy the book as much as I have.

Tom

Tom is aware of the good work the Cystic Fibrosis Trust is doing to combat this dreadful ailment and that the royalties from this publication will go a little bit more to achieve the aims of the trusts good work.

INTRODUCTION

In my early boyhood days, way back in the 1950s, my passion and dreams like millions of ambitious youngsters was to emulate our hero's of the day: Billy Wright, Tom Finney, Stanley Matthews, Bert Williams and many others.

My local football club, West Ham United who I watched on a regular basis, was buried in the middle of the old Second Division. I would marvel at the big clubs above in the then First Division: Wolverhampton Wanderers, Manchester United, Tottenham Hotspur and a football club that had a nice ring to the name – Burnley.

Still supporting them after almost sixty years people ask me the same question, why Burnley? Well it speaks for itself. They were a mighty force back then. The one game I regret not attending was the third-round FA Cup tie at White Hart Lane in that awful winter of 1963, when Burnley defeated holders Tottenham Hotspur 3–0. I did not know that the match was on because there were hundreds of cancellations that season.

At the end of the 2012–13 season, I was in the Clarets club shop looking to purchase any literature on the club, particularly history, but the closest I got was Ray Simpson's masterpiece, The Clarets Chronicles, which I had already purchased six years previously. I thought why not write my own? The history of certain players who represented Burnley over the decades would be ideal. I decided to feature the goalkeeping legends of the past and present and to include all their statistics.

I have decided to donate all profits to a charity that I am familiar with, The Cystic Fibrosis Trust, as I lost my son to this disease. It is also because at the home game against Ipswich Town at the end of the 2012–13 season, I met a young mum who was collecting for this charity. Her name is Lisa McGibbon. She lives near to the Turf Moor ground and has two sons with this condition. I spoke to her and outlined my intentions for the book I had in mind and a promise that I would get this book published.

I could not have done this without the help of certain individuals who are credited at the end of this book. Also, I must not forget the London Clarets, of whom I am a member, who have given me a platform in the past and those loyal fans who never miss a game: Pauline Pratley, Patrick O'Neill, our Chairman Ian Wood and also our magazine editors Steve Corrigan and Phil Whalley.

SENIOR COMPETITIONS

The statistics for the goalkeepers featured in this publication are as accurate as possible and include records from the following competitions:-

The Football League

The Premier League

The Football Association Challenge Cup

The Football League Cup (now the EFL Cup)

The Football League Trophy (Associate Members Cup)

European Cup

European Inter-Cities Fairs Cup

Anglo Scottish Cup

The Watney Cup

The Texaco Cup

The Football League Test Matches

The Football League Play-offs

The Football Association Charity Shield

IN THE BEGINNING

When Burnley Football Club was formed from the old Burnley Rovers Rugby Club in 1882, records were vague and inaccurate as to who scored or who played where. Most of the early football matches were friendlies and goalkeeping records were non-existent, for example, there is no record of any team selection for Burnley's record away defeat at Darwen Old Wanderers in their first FA Cup tie, which Burnley lost 11–0 in October 1885.

With the formation of the Football League in 1888, in which Burnley Football Club would proudly participate, records were kept and goalscorers logged. In the inaugural first season three goalkeepers were used in the first nine league games, Will Smith, Rob Kay and centre-forward Fred Poland who unfortunately conceded seven at Blackburn Rovers making it a total of 38 goals conceded.

To improve matters Burnley signed William Cox from Scottish club Hibernian in the month of November 1888, and he retained his goalkeeping position for the final thirteen Football League matches, conceding a total of 24 goals. Burnley Football Club ended their first Football League campaign in ninth position out of twelve, with a total of 17 points, although they had to seek re-election, for which they were thankfully, successful.

At the commencement of the following 1889–90 football season, William Cox held onto the goalkeeping position but suffered some heavy defeats, with six goals conceded at Aston Villa, followed three weeks later by a 7–1 defeat at Blackburn Rovers.

In a two week period in November of that season Burnley suffered two six goal defeats, which was followed by a record Football League defeat at Wolverhampton Wanderers 9–1. Burnley, at the foot of the table, faced huge consequences with the possibility of losing their Football League status should they seek re-election for a second year running. The Football Club decided to cross the border to Scotland where they signed a total of four new players (all forwards) with the hope of steadying the ship; William McColl, Alex Stewart, Claude Lambie and James Hill.

In the January of this campaign, goalkeeper William Cox signed for Everton and was replaced by another 'keeper from across the border, Archibald Kaye from Glasgow Thistle. Good fortune was to follow for Burnley for the rest of this season with an eleventh place finish out of twelve with 13 points. Bottom club Stoke lost their Football League status to make way for Sunderland.

ARCHIBALD KAYE
1890–91

Football League Appearances. 28

FA Cup Appearances 2

Total Goals Conceded 74

Total Clean Sheets 4

Average Conceded per Game 2.46

Archibald Kaye was born in Glasgow in 1869 and was to become one of the many players from north of the border to stabilise Burnley Football Club, who were struggling in the December of 1889 at the foot of the Football League in only their second season of participation. With the threat of possible expulsion from the Football League at the end of that campaign, Burnley's pursuit of new talent north of the border brought in players from the Glasgow area, which included Alex Stewart and William McColl from Morton, James Hill from St Mirren and centre-forward Claude Lambie from Glasgow Thistle. To complete the rebuilding a goalkeeper was prioritised; Archibald Kaye of Glasgow Thistle was offered the position of goalkeeper for Burnley Football Club in the January of 1890 as a replacement for William Cox who signed for Everton.

He made his Football League debut for Burnley on 22 February 1890 against local rivals Blackburn Rovers in a Football League fixture at Turf Moor.

In that Burnley side that afternoon were full-backs, Will Bury and Sandy Lang, with William McFetridge, Thomas White and Jack Keenan completing the half-back line. Soon to be the seasons leading scorer, Robert Haresnape was on the right wing position and the Scottish contingents William McColl, Claude Lambie, James Hill and Alex Stewart completed the forward line-up. The game ended in a 2–1 defeat for Burnley, with Alex Stewart scoring for the home side.

Burnley remained bottom of the Football League up to the final five remaining

Archie Kaye

1890 - 1891

Ron Brown

fixtures until a complete turnaround in a 7–0 defeat of Bolton Wanderers at Turf Moor, with Claude Lambie scoring his first hat-trick for the club. Although Burnley finished in eleventh place at the completion of the Football League fixtures re-election was inevitable, but re-elected they were with bottom club Stoke losing their Football League status, to be replaced by Sunderland.

Archie Kaye alongside Jack Keenan with the Lancashire Cup in 1890.

Archibald Kaye was to concede seven goals in the six games he played in his first season for the club, keeping three clean sheets. The season was to finish on a high with a beating of rivals Blackburn Rovers in the Final of the Lancashire Cup at Accrington with Archibald keeping a clean sheet in a 2–0 victory.

For the commencement of the 1890–91 Football season, Archibald was firmly installed as first choice keeper and made a total of 24 senior appearances for Burnley. This season also saw the introduction of future Burnley legends such as Walter Place senior, Billy Bowes and Tom Nicol. Burnley, with Archibald in goal, suffered some heavy defeats in that campaign, which included the seven goal deficits at Everton and Preston North End and a 6–1 defeat at Blackburn Rovers earlier in the season. Burnley completed the season in a respectable seventh position with Archibald Kaye conceding a total of 63 league goals, keeping one clean sheet.

Although this was a turning point for Burnley Football Club at the end of this 1890–91 season, which secured their status as a Football League club, it could not prevent Archibald Kaye returning back to Scotland with his whereabouts unknown.

JACK HILLMAN
1891–95 & 1898–1902

Football League Appearances. 175

FA Cup Appearances 9

Test Match Appearances 4

Total Goals Conceded 256

Total Clean Sheets 61

Average Conceded Per Game 1.36

Honours:

England International Cap 1

Goals Conceded. 2

Jack Hillman was born on 30 November 1870. His birthplace is open to question, but it is usually accepted as Calstock, Cornwall. He developed into a very large man, 6ft 4in tall with an attitude to match.

When Jack was young his parents moved to Burnley to seek employment. Jack, with his love of football, played junior football in and around the Burnley area and the junior side he was playing for were invited to play Burnley reserves due to a cancelled reserve fixture. In his position of goalkeeper he impressed the Burnley representatives that day and was offered amateur terms thereon.

In 1890 at the age of nineteen, he was signed on trial by Burnley to replace outgoing goalkeeper Archibald Kaye. He was soon in the reserves, and it was not long before he made his first team debut, which was at Accrington in a Football League fixture on 5 September 1891, which ended in a 1–0 defeat.

Also making their first team debuts that day were William Graham at inside-left and at right-back, William Jeffrey. In the centre-half position was Danny Spiers, signed from St Mirren in 1889. Alex Stewart was moved to the left-half position, with Scottish signings the previous seasons Billy Bowes at right wing,

Jack Hillman

1891 -1895
1898 - 1902

Ron Brown

at inside-right Alex McLardie and centre-forward Tom Nicol.

Interestingly this was the period that goal nets were introduced and referees and linesmen replaced umpires.

For the next four football seasons to January 1895, Jack was to be regular first team choice, missing only seven League and FA Cup ties, and Burnley over this period became a stable mid-table team.

Due to Jack Hillman's arguments and altercations with the Burnley committee, it was decided to transfer him in the January of 1895 to Everton for a fee of £200. He subsequently made his first two Everton appearances against no other than Burnley, with his old club losing both home and away matches, conceding a total of seven goals.

In March 1898 Burnley Football Club, who had been relegated the previous season, were challenging for the Second Division top spot and needed a goalkeeping replacement for outgoing Scottish 'keeper David Haddow. Jack Hillman, who was at Dundee, was asked to rejoin Burnley on the insistence of manager Harry Bradshaw, and made his second League debut for Burnley in a Second Division match at Luton Town on 19 March 1898.

Burnley won the 1897–98 Division Two title and qualified for the test matches (which they had lost in the previous season) beating Blackburn Rovers 5–1 on aggregate and drawing 0–0 with Stoke in the last match of this competition. This result was seen as dubious by many, as a draw would result in promotion for both.

In the February of 1899, Jack was selected for England against Ireland at Roker Park, Sunderland which ended in a 13–2 victory for England. It was the first occasion that an England goalkeeper was to concede a penalty. He also had the honour of representing the Football League that season.

At the end of the 1899–1900 season Burnley were in relegation trouble again and were to play Nottingham Forest on the seasons final day. It was alleged that Jack Hillman approached the Forest players with a bribe to throw the match in Burnley's favour. The Forest players rejected his offer with the club captain reporting this to the Forest committee who subsequently reported it to the Football Association Commission. Burnley lost this final League Division One match 4–0. As the old test match system had been abolished, there was no safeguard in place and Burnley were subsequently relegated. Jack was found guilty at an FA Commission hearing in Manchester and was banned from football for a twelve-month period with a fine of £300 in benefits.

After his ban he went back to Dundee, but rejoined Burnley for the commencement of the 1901–02 football season where he appeared in a total of 20 League Division Two matches before his final game for Burnley, in an FA Cup tie at Walsall, losing 1–0.

He was transferred to Manchester City where in 1904 he was in the FA Cup winning side who beat Bolton Wanderers in the Final at Crystal Palace 1—0. He moved on to Southern league side Millwall, before his goalkeeping retirement, but would eventually return to Burnley for a season as coach and for three appearances in wartime football as goalkeeper.

When he retired from football he ran a confectionery shop in Burnley. He died in December 1952.

WILLIAM TATHAM
1895–1901

Football League Appearances. 51
FA Cup Appearances 2
Total Goals Conceded 88
Total Clean Sheets 14
Average Conceded per Game 1.66

William Tatham was born in Burnley and played junior football in and around the Burnley area. It was whilst he was playing the goalkeeping roll for his local Sunday school football team that he caught the eye of representatives from Burnley Football Club. William Tatham was signed by Burnley Football Club as a professional in February of 1895.

Prior to the commencement of the 1895–96 Football League season, William Tatham was back up for new goalkeeping signing Walter Napier, who had replaced the outgoing Jack Hillman who signed for Everton.

In the first Football League match of that 1895–96 season, in an away fixture at Wolverhampton Wanderers, new goalkeeper Walter Napier suffered a serious injury on his debut. It was so serious that he was unable to fulfil his role in any future football activities and retirement was therefore imminent.

William Tatham was selected by Burnley for the following Football League fixture at West Bromwich Albion on 7 September, five days after the opening fixture at Wolverhampton, and kept a clean sheet in a 2–0 win for Burnley. In the side that day were full-backs Jeremiah Reynolds and Thomas McLintock. The halfback line up were all-rounder Walter Place senior, John Espie and Archibald Livingstone. On the wings were future leading scorer Tom Nicol and James Hill. The forwards were Billy Bowes, Walter Place junior (Walter senior's cousin) and making his debut at centre-forward was Hugh Robertson, purchased from Millwall the previous season.

Ron Brown

In his first season as goalkeeper for Burnley, William Tatham made twenty-five football league appearances and one FA Cup appearance, conceding a total of 33 goals with ten clean sheets. Burnley Football Club, under Harry Bradshaw's management, completed the 1895–96 Football League season in tenth position in a league of sixteen clubs.

The following 1896–97 season saw a lot of changes to the playing personnel with players retiring or moving to other clubs, and players of the calibre of forwards Wilf Toman and Jimmy Ross moving to the club. Although William Tatham made a total of twenty Football League appearances that season, he was subsequently dropped from the side with new signing David Haddow taking over the goalkeeping roll for the remainder of that season. Burnley Football Club finished bottom with their only hope of surviving their First Division status being a successful outcome in the test match system of the day. However, after losses in those four matches they were relegated to the Second Division of the Football League.

The successful promotion season of 1897–98, which included the dubious Test Match outcome against Stoke, didn't involve William Tatham's in any of the Second Division matches that season, although he made a brief loan spell at Bolton Wanderers before returning to Burnley.

After just two games in the 1898-99 season, William Tatham was recalled by new manager, Ernest Mangnall, for the opening home Second Division fixture on 1 September 1900 against Grimsby Town, in which he secured a clean sheet in a 3–0 win for Burnley. Another three Football League appearances were to follow with his final game for Burnley in a home fixture against Newton Heath securing a clean sheet in a 1–0 win for the home side on 15 September 1900.

He was transferred at the end of this 1900–01 season to local non-league side Nelson Football Club.

DAVID HADDOW
1896–98

Football League Appearances. 38

FA Cup Appearances 5

Total Goals Conceded 55

Total Clean Sheets 15

Test Match Appearances 4

Average Conceded per Game 1.17

Honours

Football League Division Two Championship Medal 1897–98

David Haddow was born on 12 June 1869 in Dalserf, Lanarkshire, Scotland. He started his goalkeeping career at Scottish Football Club Albion Rovers in 1888 and then made his mark in English football with Football League side Derby County in 1890, where he made sixteen goalkeeping appearances up until the end of the 1890–91 football season. After a brief spell back at Albion Rovers, he signed for Rangers for the commencement of the 1891–92 Scottish Football season. In his three-year tenure at the Glasgow club he won a Scottish Cup medal for Rangers in the 1894 Final, overcoming Celtic 3–1 at Hampden Park. In that same year he won his first and only cap for Scotland, which ended in a 2–2 drawn International against England, in Glasgow on 7 April 1894. It was whilst he was at his next Football Club Motherwell that he caught the attention of the representatives from Burnley Football Club, and signed for them in December 1895.

With first choice keeper William Tatham unable to play in the FA Cup home match against Stoke on 18 February 1896, David Haddow was selected for this tie which ended in a 1–1 drawn game. The replay took place five days later on 20 February at Stoke and ended in a 7–1 defeat for Burnley with the single Burnley goal scored by Billy Bowes.

David Haddow

1896 - 1898

Ron Brown

David Haddow made a total of six senior appearances for Burnley that season and the club ended with a tenth place finish in the league.

Although David Haddow was understudy to first choice 'keeper William Tatham for the 1896–97 Football season, he managed to represent Burnley in ten of those First Division fixtures, which ended with Burnley having finished bottom and having to qualify for their First Division status through the Test Match system. David Haddow was duly selected for the four matches that were played in the April of 1897. Two defeats and a draw, with just one victory, was not enough to prevent Burnley being relegated to the Second Division of English Football.

David Haddow was to play a major part in the promotion season of 1897–98 and was selected for the first twenty-four Second Division fixtures, but played his final game for Burnley at Turf Moor on 12 March 1898 in a Second Division fixture against Gainsborough Trinity which ended in a 1–1 draw.

With the return of Jack Hillman from Dundee he was no longer needed. He signed for New Brighton where he made thirty-four appearances and in 1899 signed for Southern League club Tottenham Hotspur, where he was to make twenty-eight appearances up to the end of 1901.

HENRY COLLINS
1900–01

Football League Appearances. 30

FA Cup Appearance 3

Total Goals Conceded 28

Total Clean Sheets 15

Average Conceded per Game 0.85

Henry Collins was born in Winlaton, County Durham in 1876, and played for Northern Alliance non-league club Hebburn Argyle, near Gateshead, Co Durham. Burnley Football Club, in their pursuit of players from the North East of England, were attracted by Henry Collins' talent and he was offered professional terms, which he duly signed in June 1900.

Burnley, who were relegated the previous 1899–1900 season, now made all working decisions on and off the field through a select committee after the resignation of manager Harry Bradshaw.

With the absence of suspended goalkeeper Jack Hillman for the entire season, a goalkeeper was the priority with William Tatham returning for the first four Football League fixtures of the 1900–01 campaign. Henry Collins was selected for the Second Division fixture at previously relegated Glossop on 22 September 1900, which ended with a 1–0 win for Burnley.

Also making his debut that day was William Howarth at inside-left who was purchased from Accrington. The full-back line up consisted of new pre-season signings James Lindsay and George Lockhart: a formidable half-back line, consisting of future England half-back Billy Bannister with Fred Barron and captain Joe Taylor. On the wings were Thomas Morrison and James Sutherland with the other inside forwards William Watkins and Billy Bowes.

Henry Collins was now the first choice selection for the remainder of the 1900–

Henry Collins

1900-1901

Ron Brown

01 football season and never conceded more than three goals on any one occasion. In the thirty-three senior matches that he played he conceded a total of only 28 goals and secured fifteen clean sheets.

Burnley who were top of this division numerous times throughout that campaign, missing promotion by six points to finish in third spot. Henry Collins' record that season was truly remarkable for a first year's introduction into the Football League, with fewer than one goal a game conceded.

With Jack Hillman returning to the fray for the following 1901–02 football season, London non-league club Queens Park Rangers were interested in securing the signature of Henry Collins and the new Burnley Manager, Ernest Mangnall, duly accepted the offer from the London side.

Over the four-year period at Rangers he made over 100 appearances and at the commencement of the 1905–06 football season he signed for Everton, where he made three senior appearances, with his debut for the First Division side in October 1905.

WILLIAM GREEN
1903–08

Football League Appearances. 147

FA Cup Appearances 6

Total Goals Conceded 222

Total Clean Sheets 44

Average Conceded per Game 1.45

William John Green was born in Gravesend, Kent in 1882 and started his early goalkeeping career playing for his local junior side eventually signing for West London non-league club Brentford. He was well built, over 6ft tall, and was known for his safe handling and agility. Burnley Football Club who finished bottom of the Second Division the previous 1902–03 season and narrowly won re-election, needed urgent replacements which William Green was to be one of.

He signed for Burnley Football Club in the summer of 1903. He made his Football League debut on the opening day of the 1903–04 season at Chesterfield on 5 September 1903, keeping a clean sheet in a 0–0 drawn game.

Making their debuts that day were centre-half David Walders, signed from Barrow, Thomas Aspden at outside-right, Dugald McFarlane at centre-forward, William Jackson at inside-left and at outside-left Henry Williams. Making up the full-back line were Henry Ross and William Jenkinson returning for a second spell from West Ham United. The other half-backs were Fred Barron at right-half and Arthur Dixon at left-half. The other remaining forward at inside-right was James Crawford.

Green played a total of four games without conceding a goal until his fifth game at Preston North End where he conceded in the thirteenth minute. In his first full season at Burnley he made a total of 35 league and Cup appearances, but suffered

William Green

1903 - 1908

Ron Brown

a six goal defeat at Glossop. In his second season, in a league match at Chesterfield he was to become one of only ten players to have taken the field that day due to full-back Hugh Moffat missing his train connection at Manchester

In the 1904–05 season he played a total of 445 minutes without conceding a league goal from 11 February 1905 till 1 April 1905. He became regular goalkeeper

33

up until the end of the 1906–07 campaign and in his four season spell missed only three games for Burnley.

After four Football League matches at the commencement of the 1907–08 season William Green was dropped from the side to be replaced by a future Burnley goalkeeping legend, Jerry Dawson. He made a couple of goalkeeping appearances up until 17 October 1908, when Burnley entertained Fulham in a 3–1 home defeat, that being his last. He was transferred to Bradford Park Avenue and made a total of 31 appearances before retiring from football.

During the Great War he saw active service and was seriously injured and left disabled. He became a regular visitor to Turf Moor during the 1920s.

JERRY DAWSON
1907–1928

Football League Appearances. 522

FA Cup Appearances 45

Football Association Charity Shield 1

Total Goals Conceded 794

Total Clean Sheets 164

Average Conceded Per Game 1.40

Honours:

FA Cup (didn't play in the final though) 1914

First Division Runners-Up Medal. 1919-20

Football League Championship Medal 1920–21

Second Division Runners-Up Medal 1912–13

England International Caps 2

Goals conceded 2

Jeremiah (Jerry) Dawson was born the third son of Thomas Dawson in the village of Cliviger, Lancashire on 18 March 1888 and was to play for Burnley Football Club over a twenty-year period.

When Jerry left school he became an apprentice blacksmith in his home village and played junior football in his favoured goalkeeping position for Portsmouth Rovers. Having caught the attention of the representatives from Burnley with his goalkeeping ability and talent, he was offered a trial with the club. At only eighteen years of age, he made his debut for the reserves against St Helens Town before finally signing professional terms in February 1907.

Within two months on 13 April he made his first team debut for Burnley Football Club at Turf Moor against Stockport County, which ended in a 3-0 win. In that side were legendary players that included Fred Barron at right-back and

Arthur Dixon at left-half. In the forward line, at inside-left was amateur player and local architect Arthur Bell. This was to be Jerry's only game that season as first choice 'keeper William Green was recalled to the side, which finished the Football League Second Division in seventh place under manager Spen Whittaker.

After four games at the start of the 1907–08 season William Green was finally dropped with Jerry taking over the first team goalkeeping position at Hull City, which ended in a 3–1 defeat for the men in green shirts. He was to make a total of 34 Football League Division Two appearances that season, conceding 41 goals and keeping 10 clean sheets, with Spen's men finishing in seventh position for the second year running.

Having now established a first choice goalkeeping position, tragedy was to befall Burnley Football Club at the end of April 1910 with the loss of manager Spen Whittaker, who fell from a train just outside Crewe while on his way to London to register a player for the following days fixture against Manchester City. The club remained managerless until July 1910 when they appointed former Accrington club secretary, John Haworth, who was to make a tremendous impact on the club, firstly changing the club colours from green to claret and blue.

In a FA Cup quarter-final match at Bradford City on 11 March 1911, in front of a record crowd of 39,146, Burnley lost to a single goal when Jerry Dawson went up for a high cross. He subsequently lost control of the ball, which then ended up in the back of the net. Bradford City went on to win the FA Cup that season beating Newcastle United in the Final.

In the 1912–13 promotion winning season, Jerry Dawson was dropped for the first time for two games, but was back to his best as Burnley went eleven winning games in succession in all competitions (which is still unbroken) from 16 November 1912 to 18 January 1913.

On 1 February 1913 Burnley, who had beaten Gainsborough Trinity in the FA Cup, signed Borough keeper Ron Sewell (along with their two full-backs) as back up for Jerry. He was given six first team appearances that season which ended with promotion back to the First Division of the Football League and a FA Cup semi-final, losing to Sunderland 3–2.

Burnley made a great impact in their first season back and made it once again to the semi-finals of the FA Cup, with Sheffield United their opponents. In a 0–0 drawn tie at Old Trafford Jerry suffered an injury that prevented him from playing the replayed game at Goodison Park, where Ron Sewell deputised, and a goal from skipper Tommy Boyle took Burnley to their first FA Cup Final at Crystal Palace on 25 April 1914. Jerry Dawson returned for the Football League match three weeks later at Manchester City, but was once again injured and unable to finish the full ninety minutes with full-back David Taylor taking over. The Cup Final beckoned with Jerry Dawson having to decide, 'Shall I play or shouldn't I play?' Being a true sportsman, a gentleman and a very honest man, he decided to step down and give Ron Sewell the position of goalkeeper for the final tie, which ended with Burnley winning by a single goal scored by Bert Freeman.

In the final season before the outbreak of the First World War, Jerry Dawson made a total of thirty-eight League and Cup appearances with Burnley finishing in fourth place with 43 points.

During the hostilities of war Jerry joined the forces, along with hundreds of other professional footballers, but managed to play regional matches for Burnley when available and made a total of 78 appearances.

When football resumed for the commencement of the 1919–20 season Burnley, with Jerry Dawson back in goal, finished their first season in second place on 51 points behind champions West Bromwich Albion. New faces to the side were full-back Len Smelt, centre-forward Joe Anderson and left-winger Walter Weaver. That season Bradford Park Avenue visited Turf Moor and put six goals into Jerry Dawson's net, but Burnley returned to Park Avenue seven days later, winning the game 1–0. Jerry Dawson was injured once again against Oldham Athletic, and Ron Sewell again deputised for an eight-match spell. Once Jerry had regained full fitness Ron Sewell decided that he no longer wanted reserve football and was transferred to local rivals Blackburn Rovers.

The following 1920–21 football season was to see Burnley Football Club make history with a record 30 league games played without defeat. The Football League First Division was won with a total of 59 points with a team consisting of Burnley legends, Halley, Boyle and Watson, forwards Benny Cross, and Bob Kelly, and winger Eddie Mosscrop with club top scorer Joe Anderson netting 25 goals.

The following 1921–22 season was Jerry Dawson's finest at Burnley with the honour of being selected for England against Ireland on 22 October 1921 in Belfast, this being the first of his two caps. The second being for the home International against Scotland at Villa Park on 8 April 1922, which consisted of future Burnley manager Tom Bromilow playing in the England side. He remained consistent in the Burnley side, which included an FA Cup semi-final place in March 1924 which they lost 3–0 to Aston Villa.

In 1925–26 season the offside rules of the game were changed and Burnley at the start of this season didn't condition themselves to the changes. In the opening fixture at Villa Park 10 goals were conceded, with many more to follow including eight at Manchester City.

In the 1926–27 season George Sommerville was signed as replacement for an ageing Jerry Dawson who made just one appearance that season

His final appearance for Burnley was against Liverpool at Turf Moor on 25 December 1928, which ended in a 3–2 win for the home side. From the green of Burnley in 1907 to the claret and blue of the present, under three managers Jerry Dawson's record is unbeaten and likely to remain so.

After retiring from football he took up coaching and played cricket for Burnley Cricket Club. On November 2011 a memorial plaque was unveiled in his home town of Clivigar in his memory. He died in 1970.

RON SEWELL
1913–20

Football League Appearances. 23

FA Cup Appearances 4

Total Goals Conceded 37

Total Clean Sheets 10

Average Conceded per Game 1.37

Honours

FA Cup Winners Medal 1913–14

Ronald W. Sewell was born in Middlesbrough on 19 July 1890. He played his early football for Gainsborough Trinity as a junior before moving back to the North East, signing for Wingate Albion in the North Eastern League in 1910.

The following 1911–12 season he re-signed for Gainsborough Trinity who ended that season bottom of the Football League Division Two and relegation followed.

Gainsborough Trinity, now a non-league side, were drawn to play Burnley in the second round of the FA Cup at Turf Moor on 1 February 1913, a side that included players of the calibre of half-backs Tommy Boyle and Billy Watson and legendary forward Bert Freeman. The final outcome was a 4–1 home victory for Burnley, but it did not quite end there. Three players in the 'Borough side, goalkeeper Ron Sewell and full-backs Sam Gunton and Cliff Jones, impressed the Burnley representatives enough for the trio to be signed for the club ninety minutes after this tie was completed. On 8 February, seven days later, the three players made their Football League debuts at Bristol City, which ended in a 3–3 drawn game. Goalkeeper Ron Sewell played a further five league games that 1912–13 campaign with left-back Cliff Jones establishing himself in that position for a further seven seasons, but unfortunately, right-back Sam Gunton never played for Burnley again; choosing to join the armed forces instead. Ron Sewell was signed

Ron Sewell
1913-1920

Ron Brown

originally as back up for Burnley goalkeeping legend Jerry Dawson. Burnley finished the season as runners-up to Preston North End, gaining promotion back to the top flight after an absence of thirteen years.

With Burnley progressing well in their return to First Division football, Ron Sewell was to be called upon, due to an injury to first choice 'keeper Jerry Dawson, for an FA Cup semi-final replay at Goodison Park against Sheffield United. With Ron Sewell keeping a clean sheet in the replay, Burnley were eventually through to their first FA Cup Final. Ron Sewell, after a further four league appearances, was replaced by a now injury recovered Jerry Dawson for the away fixture at Manchester City. Once again Jerry Dawson suffered a reoccurrence of his injury and was unable to continue in this game, with the Final tie at Crystal Palace only seven days away. With Dawson declining to play in the Final, Ron Sewell was elected to represent Burnley Football Club on this historic day, with Burnley taking the Cup back to Lancashire and Ron Sewell becoming part of this triumphant side.

The football season prior to the outbreak of World War One resulted in Ron Sewell appearing just three times.

Throughout the war Ron served as a gunner in the Royal Garrison Artillery and also, like many other players of that day, guested for Grimsby Town and Lincoln City.

With the recommencement of League football in the 1919–20 campaign, Ron Sewell was to make a further ten football appearances which included two FA Cup ties, his last being in a Football League fixture at Sheffield Wednesday on 24 January. In February 1920 he had decided that he was not prepared to play any further as back-up to first choice 'keeper Jerry Dawson, and was transferred to local rivals Blackburn Rovers on the thirteenth of that month.

He was to make 227 Football League appearances for Blackburn and on 3 March 1924 was selected for England against Wales at Ewood Park in a British Championship match, which Wales became the victors of in a 2–1 win. He retired from football with Blackburn Rovers in September 1927, but Gainsborough Trinity persuaded him to rejoin them for a third time soon after.

After his final retirement from football he, like many other retired sportsmen, took up what was an aptly named occupation, a licenced victualler and ran a public house in Lincoln. He died on 4 February 1945.

GEORGE SOMMERVILLE
1926–32

Football League Appearances. 118

FA Cup Appearances 6

Total Goals Conceded 265

Total Clean Sheets 18

Average Conceded per Game 2.14

Goalkeeper George Douglas Liddle Sommerville was born in Glasgow in 1901. Burnley Football Club, who under manager Albert Pickles, narrowly missed relegation in the 1925–26 Football League Division One season, were in urgent need of a goalkeeping replacement for an ageing Jerry Dawson. Their pursuit of a goalkeeping replacement led them north of the border to Scotland where George Sommerville, Hamilton Academical's 'keeper fitted their requirements. George Sommerville was signed by Burnley in July 1926 in time for the commencement of the new Football League season.

Sommerville was to be Burnley's only serious pre-season signing, and was selected for the opening Football League Division One home game against Cardiff City on 28 August 1926. In the side that day were full-backs Andy McCluggage and Fred Blinkhorn, the half-back line up consisted of England International Jack Hill at centre-half with John Steel and William Dougall taking up the other positions. The wingers, both future England Internationals, consisted of Jack Bruton and double hat-trick hero of the previous season Louis Page. Burnley veteran Benny Cross was at inside-right, goal scoring legend George Beel at centre-forward with Harold Hargreaves at inside-left. The opening fixture was a 4–3 home win for Burnley with Harold Hargreaves netting twice.

George Sommerville was to make a total of 41 Football League appearances that season, but conceded a total of 82 goals in all competitions. It was certainly

George Sommerville

1926 - 1932

Ron Brown

a complete turnaround to the previous season with Pickles men finishing in a healthy fifth place position in this 1926–27 football season.

After 13 Football League starts to the following 1927-28 campaign, Sommerville lost his place due to a collar bone injury that prevented him competing for the remainder of this season. This was also the season that George Beel broke Bert

Freeman's 1912 goal scoring record with 35 Football League goals that remains a club record to this day.

George Sommerville was to make only four Football League appearances the following 1928–29 season which followed the final appearance on Christmas Day of Burnley goalkeeping legend Jerry Dawson. He conceded a total of 20 goals in these four matches, eight at Liverpool and a record ten goals at Sheffield United, keeping a total of one clean sheet. William Down played the remaining 16 Football League fixtures and was now the clubs first choice goalkeeper.

With the very serious injury that William Down sustained at Blackburn Rovers on 9 November 1929, George Sommerville was recalled to the side for the remainder of the season that finally finished with Burnley being relegated back to the Second Division of the Football League after an absence of 17 years.

Herman Conway was purchased in the February of that 1929–30 season as replacement for Down, plus back up for Sommerville

Burnley Football Club made two changes to the side for the commencement of the 1930–31 Football League Division Two season, with the signing of winger Evan Jenkins from Lincoln City and Billy Mays from Notts County. There was to be a rude awakening for their introduction to League Two status with the 8–1 thumping at Tottenham in only the clubs second Football League game: certainly a bad start for George Sommerville who was subsequently dropped after six games to be replaced by previous seasons signing Herman Conway. Sommerville was recalled to the side the following February for seven league matches, but once again dropped in favour of Herman Conway's return. Burnley finished the season in eighth position on 45 points, with a total of 79 goals conceded in all competitions.

At the start of the 1931–32 campaign their were no changes for the opening game at Southampton, with Conway taking up the goalkeeping position, but he was subsequently dropped after this 3–0 away defeat. George Sommerville was recalled to the side for the next seventeen Football League matches, but conceded 18 goals in the final four games. Once again Sommerville was dropped to make way for amateur goalkeeper Richard Twist, who the previous month was signed from non-league side Hindsford, but was recalled for a couple of league games and dropped once again after a 4–1 home defeat by Oldham Athletic on 27 February 1932.

This was to be his final game for Burnley after a six-season spell. The season for Burnley ended with them narrowly avoiding relegation to the third tier by two points with a nineteenth position finish. It was to be that season legends George Beel and Louis Page were transferred to Lincoln City and Manchester United respectively. Although George Sommerville was to concede a large number of goals, he was only as good as his defence at the time.

He was transferred to Bristol City where he made a total of 34 appearances before playing non-league football and retiring from the game.

WILLIAM DOWN
1927–29

Football League Appearances. 80

FA Cup Appearances 2

Total Goals Conceded 185

Total Clean Sheets 11

Average Conceded per Game 2.26

William Down was born on 22 January 1898 in Ryhope near Sunderland and was an experienced goalkeeping veteran when he joined Burnley Football Club, who needed a backup for now reserve 'keeper and Burnley goalkeeping legend Jerry Dawson. He started his playing career at Leeds United, who were in the Second Division of the Football League and was part of Leeds United promotion to the First Division in 1924, with 36 League and Cup appearances. He made a total of ninety-six senior goalkeeping appearances at Leeds United before being transferred to Yorkshire rivals Doncaster Rovers then in the Third Division North of the Football League.

In his two seasons with the club he made a total of over fifty appearances before Burnley offered him reserve football and he signed for the club in September 1927 with the football season now underway. With the injury to first choice 'keeper George Sommerville, sustained in a 7–1 defeat at Bolton for Burnley, meant that a replacement would urgently be required for the following Saturdays visit of Birmingham. Jerry Dawson's unavailability also gave William Down his opportunity and his Burnley debut at Turf Moor on 12 November 1927.

A few familiar faces were to appear in the team line-up, which included England International George Waterfield at left-back and new signing from East Fife, Jim Brown, with Jack Hill and George Parkin making up the half-back line-up. Wingers were Jack Bruton and Louis Page, with Albert Freeman, George Beel

Billy Down

1927 - 1930

Ron Brown

and Joe Devine making up the other forward positions. The game ended with a 2–1 victory for Burnley, with a goal each from George Beel and Albert Freeman. William Down was now officially first choice goalkeeper with a total of thirty senior appearances for the season.

Burnley Football Club once again narrowly avoided relegation that 1927–28 season, which recorded 98 league goals that were conceded by both goalkeepers, William Down and George Sommerville, but was also the season that George Beel set his goal scoring record of 35 league goals.

In the following 1928–29 campaign he was selected for First Team duties up till Christmas Day, when goalkeeping legend Jerry Dawson made his swan song at Turf Moor against Liverpool in a 3–2 win for Burnley. A hand injury in the previous game at Arsenal kept Billy Down out of the side for several weeks with George Sommerville taking over his goalkeeping duties. He returned for the FA Cup fixture at Swindon Town, but Burnley came away beaten 3–2 by the men from Wiltshire. He made a total of thirty-seven Football League appearances that season, but conceded heavily at Cardiff City and Huddersfield Town, with a seven goal deficit at both early in that season. Burnley once again finished in nineteenth position, narrowly avoiding relegation for a second year in succession.

With the start of the 1929–30 season, there were no early changes to the playing side for the first fixture at Manchester City, which ended in a 2–2 drawn match. Burnley Football Club, with Down in goal, were once again struggling near the bottom end of the First Division. In the fifth match of the season at Highbury, Burnley lost 6–1 to an up and coming Arsenal side.

The away trip to rivals Blackburn Rovers at Ewood Park on 9 November 1929 was to be met in tragic circumstances for goalkeeper William Down, when he went into a challenge with Rovers forward Wilf Crompton. He was badly injured in the collision, but bravely carried on with Rovers taking full advantage of the situation, beating Burnley 8–3. After the game Billy Down collapsed and was rushed to a nearby hospital where he was diagnosed with a ruptured kidney and was fortunate to have survived.

He never recovered his fitness for first class football and was released by Burnley at the end of that football season, which also ended Burnley's First Division status and they were relegated along with Everton. Before retiring from football he played for Wigan Borough and Torquay United. His death is undocumented.

HERMAN CONWAY
1930–34

Football League Appearances. 81

FA Cup Appearances 6

Total Goals Conceded 148

Total Clean Sheets 16

Average Conceded per Game 1.70

Herman Conway was born in Gainsborough, Lincolnshire on 11 October 1908. In his early football career he played for his local football side Gainsborough Trinity, who were in the Midland League. He made a brief ten-month appearance with the club from March 1929 and was spotted by former Burnley goalkeeping legend Jerry Dawson, who was now scouting for new talent.

Herman Conway was introduced to Burnley Football Club in February 1930 and duly signed for the club as back up for first choice 'keeper George Sommerville. He was to be the second goalkeeper to be signed from Gainsborough Trinity at that time; the other being Ronnie Sewell who signed for Burnley in 1913 seventeen years previously.

Burnley, who at the commencement of the 1930–31 season were now a Second Division side and struggling to attract the crowds, made a goalkeeping change for the clubs Football League Division Two fixture at Wolverhampton Wanderers with the introduction of Herman Conway's debut. In the Burnley side for this fixture on 20 September 1930 were full-backs Andy McCluggage and George Waterfield, the half-back line-up consisted of Jim Brown, Peter O'Dowd and Harry Storer: on the wings were Evan Jenkins and Louis Page with George Beel. Joe Mantle and Thomas Prest the other inside-forwards. The outcome of the match was a 4–2 win for Burnley, with Louis Page scoring two of the goals.

Herman Conway was now firmly installed as Burnley first choice goalkeeper

Herman Conway

1930 - 1934

Ron Brown

for the remainder of the season, barring seven league appearances from George Sommerville, and made a total of thirty-one senior appearances in the 1930–31 season.

After only one appearance at the start of the following football season at Southampton, Herman Conway was dropped from the side to be replaced once again by previous first choice 'keeper George Sommerville, but was reinstated back to the side following Sommerville's demotion for the trip to Bury on 5 March 1932. A lot of new faces were to appear for that fixture, with a total of five changes from the first fixture at Southampton, Burnley were to finish the season in nineteenth position, two points off relegation, in only their second league season back in the second tier.

The following 1932–33 campaign started well, although a 6–1 away defeat at Preston North End didn't bode well, with Conway making the goalkeeping position his own for the first eleven Division Two fixtures. New manger Tom Bromilow decided to change the goalkeeping position and Conway was replaced for the fixture at West Ham United by locally born new signing from Clitheroe, Charles Hillam, who conceded four goals in a drawn match. The goalkeeping position that season was more or less shared between Conway and Hillam, who went on to sign for Manchester United, with Conway contributing twenty-five senior appearances. The football season once again finished as the previous year in nineteenth position.

Burnley Football Club made another pre-season signing with goalkeeper Alex Scott from Liverpool who more or less shared the goalkeeping position for the start of the 1933–34 season with Conway. Another new goalkeeper, Tom Hetherington, was signed from North East junior side Walker Celtic at the end of 1933 and this made Herman Conway redundant after his final game at Turf Moor against Manchester United on 3 February 1934 after conceding 4 goals in a 4–1 home defeat. Burnley finished the football season in twelfth place, which was an improvement on the previous two seasons.

Herman Conway signed for West Ham United at the end of that season and made numerous appearances for the Second Division club, which included the victory against Blackburn Rovers at Wembley in the war time Cup Final of 1940.

He made sixteen appearances for Burnley Football Club during the war as a guest player and signed for Southend United when hostilities ceased in 1946 before finally retiring from football.

ALEX SCOTT
1933–36

Football League Appearances. 57

FA Cup Appearances 8

Total Goals Conceded 101

Total Clean Sheets 17

Average Conceded per Game 1.55

Robert Alexander Scott was born in Liverpool on 29 October 1913. In his early goalkeeping career he joined Liverpool Football Club and was a member of their ground staff. He unfortunately was unable to gain recognition and was overlooked with regards to a playing career there.

He was very tall at six foot four inches and a good handler of the ball, which attracted Burnley manager Tom Bromilow to sign him as cover for first choice 'keeper Herman Conway in May 1933.

Five games into the 1933–34 season at Upton Park for the Second Division fixture against West Ham United on 9 September, Alex Scott was selected for his goalkeeping debut for Burnley in place of Conway. In the Burnley side that day was Thomas Willigan and George Waterfield at full-backs. The half-back selection consisted of Ray Bennion, George Bellis and Jim brown. The two wingers were Bill Sellars and John Mustard and making up the remaining forward line-up were Eddie Hancock, Cyril Smith and Harry O'Grady. The result ended with a 2–1 win for Burnley with goals scored from Eddie Hancock and Cyril Smith.

Throughout this football season there were three goalkeepers challenging for the number one spot, with games restricted due to the signing of Tom Hetherington late in December 1933. Alex Scott managed to play a total of eleven Football League matches that first season, which Burnley finished in thirteenth position.

At the commencement of the following 1934–35 campaign, he was selected

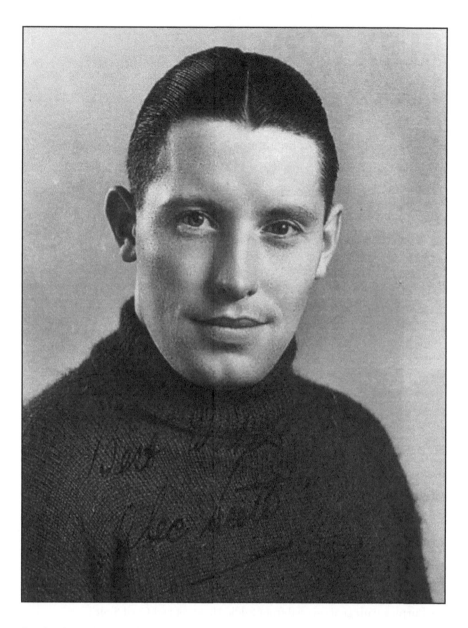

for the first nine Football League fixtures which included five new signings for Burnley. He made a total of 34 senior appearances that season, in which Burnley reached the semi-final of the FA Cup where they met eventual winners Sheffield Wednesday which ended in a 3–0 defeat at Villa Park. In the league Burnley could only finish one better from the previous season where they finished twelfth.

He was to concede quite heavily at Brentford, who scored six against him, and another seven at Bolton Wanderers where both clubs gained promotion that season. Interestingly enough Alex Scott also conceded five goals at Brentford the previous season. He was subsequently dropped for the final nine Football League matches and the first nine also for the commencement of the 1935–36 season.

He was selected for the Football League fixture at Tottenham Hotspur, but this ended with Alex conceding five goals on his return. Although this was a set back, he was to make a further eighteen consecutive appearances for Burnley when Wolverhampton Wanderers made a formal offer of £1,250 for Alex Scott's services. This offer was accepted by Burnley Football Club, who were now without a manager and run by a selection committee. His final game for Burnley was where it all started at Upton Park on the 3 February 1936 against West Ham United, which ended in a goalless draw.

He made his Football League Division One debut for Wolverhampton Wanderers the following week and kept a clean sheet in a 0–0 drawn match against Derby County. He was a member of the Wolverhampton Wanderers side that finished as runners up in the First Division of 1937–38 and 1938–39. The pinnacle of his career was a Cup Final appearance against Portsmouth at Wembley in 1939 that ended in a 4–1 defeat for Wolves.

During hostilities of the Second World War, Alex Scott made eighty-five appearances for Wolves and was a guest player for Aston Villa and Southport. When league football returned in 1946 Wolverhampton Wanderers and England legend Bert Williams replaced Scott, who was transferred to Crewe Alexandra where he made forty-four appearances for them over a two-season spell.

When he retired from football he ran a general store in Wolverhampton and later joined the local police force. He died in 1962.

TOM HETHERINGTON
1934–37

Football League Appearances. 67

FA Cup Appearances 0

Total Goals Conceded 105

Total Clean Sheets 16

Average Conceded per Game. 1.57

Thomas Burns Hetherington was born in Walker, Newcastle Upon Tyne on 22 January 1911. He started his goalkeeping career with his local junior side Walker Celtic in 1933, who were at the time a semi-professional football club playing in the North Eastern League. With Burnley's pursuit of football playing staff in the North East of England, they spotted Tom Hetherington's ability in the goalkeeping position at Walker, and he was offered reserve team football as understudy to present goalkeepers Alex Scott and Herman Conway and terms were agreed in late December 1933.

On 10 February 1934, manager Tom Bromilow decided as a matter of urgency to give Tom Hetherington his debut in a Second Division match at Bolton Wanderers, with Burnley in seventeenth position and the prospect of facing relegation a possibility. With Hetherington in goal the full-backs were Gilbert Richmond and Wilfred Smith. The half-back line-up consisted of Jim Brown, George Bellis and Alick Robinson. The wingers were Eddie Hancock and Tom Weale, with Arthur Warburton, Cyril Smith and Thomas Douglas making up the forward line-up. Burnley came away from the game with a 4–1 defeat with the only Burnley goal scored by Arthur Warburton. Although this was a set back to his Burnley career, Tom Hetherington was selected for the final fifteen league fixtures for this 1933–34 season, with Burnley Football Club securing their Second Division status with a thirteenth place finish.

Tom Hetherington

1934 - 1937

Ron Brown

The season ended in heartbreak for ex Burnley player and trainer Charlie Bates, who was not retained by the club after being a loyal servant for 24 years.

The following 1934–35 season, Alex Scott was selected for first team goalkeeping duties for the first nine Second Division fixtures with Tom Hetherington taking over the next five fixtures. He was to make a total of fourteen appearances to the end of that season, with Burnley finishing in twelfth position.

The 1935–36 season was to see a change in the selection process (and a change from claret and blue to a black and white strip) with manager Tom Bromilow being replaced by a selection committee. Tom Hetherington was given the first choice goalkeeping position for the first nine Second Division fixtures of that season and once again was dropped in favour of Alex Scott, who played the rest of that season but for two fixtures that Tom Hetherington undertook. Burnley once again finished the season in thirteenth position.

The commencement of the 1936–37 season was to be Tom Hetherington's best for Burnley, with him being now officially first choice 'keeper for the first twenty-four Football League games. In this Burnley side was a young forward named Tommy Lawton who was to make his name for various other top football clubs as well as international duties with England. Although Hetherington was dropped from the side to make way for Ted Adams, he was to suffer a heavy defeat at Leicester City in that season which ended in a 7–3 beating for Burnley. Once again Burnley finished that season in thirteenth position.

The following season he played just one more time for Burnley in a home Second Division fixture against Bradford Park Avenue on 4 December 1937, which ended in a 1–1 drawn match.

Throughout his time at Burnley he was never selected for any cup games. He was released by Burnley following his final game and returned to the North East to play for non-league Jarrow. In 1939 he was signed by Barnsley, but did not make any appearances for them and returned to Burnley as a guest player, where he made one appearance during the hostilities of the Second World War.

From 1946–47 he joined Gateshead of the Third Division North and made one appearance for them before retiring from football. It is believed he died on 1 January 1968 but there is little documentary evidence of this.

TED ADAMS
1936–39

Football League Appearances. 111

FA Cup Appearances   7

Total Goals Conceded 164

Total Clean Sheets 36

Average Conceded per Game 1.39

Edward Fairclough Adams was born in Anfield, Liverpool on 30 November 1906. His early playing career consisted of junior football in the local Lancashire Leagues before catching the attention of Liverpool Football Club at the age of 21 and was offered terms, which he duly signed in February 1927. Like his predecessor Alex Scott, he was unable to obtain a goalkeeping selection with the club and moved on to several non-league sides before eventually landing the goalkeeping position at Third Division North side Wrexham in 1931. He made eighty-nine appearances for the Welsh side before moving on to Southport in 1935 where he made thirteen appearances.

With Alex Scott's transfer to Wolverhampton Wanderers in February 1936 a replacement goalkeeper was needed as back up for Tom Hetherington. Ted Adams, who had incidentally retired from football at the time, was invited to consider returning and was persuaded by the Burnley selection committee to accept the offer that was given and he duly signed as a member of the playing staff of Burnley Football Club.

His debut for Burnley came suddenly and at the age of 29 on 29 February 1936, in a home Second Division fixture against West Ham United, he took up the goalkeeping position. In that Burnley side were full-backs George Nevin and Henry Hubbick. The half-back line consisted of John Hindmarsh, Robert Johnson and club captain Alick Robinson. On the wings were Thomas Storey and

Ted Adams

1936 - 1939

Ron Brown

Charlie Fletcher with Eddie Hancock, Cyril Smith and Ron Hornby making up the forward line. The result was a 1–0 win for Burnley with a goal scored by Ron Hornby.

He played twelve of the thirteen final games for Burnley to the end of that 1935–36 season, with Burnley finishing in thirteenth position.

At the commencement of the 1936–37 Football League season Ted Adams was now reserve and understudy to Tom Hetherington. On 9 January 1937 Ted Adams was selected for the League Division Two game at Aston Villa keeping a clean sheet in a 0–0 drawn match. He made a total of sixteen league appearances to the end of this campaign, plus three FA Cup appearances that included the 7–1 demolition by Arsenal at Turf Moor in the fifth round of the FA Cup. Burnley's league performance was as the previous season, a mid-table thirteenth position finish.

For the next two football seasons before the outbreak of World War Two Ted Adams was to secure his first team selection and make a total of eighty-three Football League plus four FA Cup appearances. Burnley finished the 1937–38 season in a respectable sixth position, but were back the following season in the usual mid-table position of fourteenth.

At the start of the 1939–40 league season Ted Adams was once again first choice 'keeper, but due to the outbreak of war only two Second Division matches were played (Coventry City at home and Birmingham away) and were voided. Although Ted Adams was not involved in combat throughout the hostilities, he made a total of nineteen goalkeeping appearances for Burnley, which were mostly made up of friendlies. He made several guest appearances for other clubs including New Brighton and Wrexham, before finally retiring in 1943 at the age of 37.

JIMMY STRONG
1946–52

Football League Appearances. 264

FA Cup Appearances 21

Total Goals Conceded 294

Total Clean Sheets 103

Average Conceded per Game 1.03

Honours:

FA Cup Runners-up Medal   1946–47

Second Division Runners-up Medal   1946–47

James G. Strong was born in Morpeth, Northumberland on 7 June 1916, and was to become one of the all-time goalkeeping greats at Burnley Football Club. In his early youth he played junior football as a full-back for local sides Pegswood Villa and Choppington Welfare before adopting the position of goalkeeper. In 1934, at the age of 18, he was spotted by Football League side Hartlepools United and duly signed for them on professional terms. He made his debut against local rivals Gateshead in the February of that 1933–34 season, ending in a 3–3 drawn match.

The following summer of 1934 he attracted the attention of Third Division South side Chesterfield and signed for them on a free transfer where he made a total of twenty-one consecutive appearances before eventually signing for First Division side Portsmouth in March 1935. He made sixty-two League and Cup appearances at Portsmouth before having a brief spell at Southern League side Gillingham and subsequently moving to Third Division South side Walsall before the hostilities of the Second World War. He joined the RAF and made several guest appearances for Blackpool, Rochdale and finally Burnley where he made 103 appearances.

Burnley FC line up in the 1951 / 1952 season

In May 1945 Burnley Football Club appointed their first full-time manager in over ten years with the arrival of former England half-back Cliff Britton. His first competitive games were the two-legged FA Cup ties against Stoke City with two goalkeepers, George Foxcroft and Jack Breedon, representing Burnley in both of these FA Cup ties. Jimmy Strong, who was still on Walsall's books, was offered the goalkeeping position at Burnley and an offer to Walsall of £450 for his services was duly accepted.

Many new signings were made prior to the commencement of the 1946–47 Football League season, which included Alan Brown from Huddersfield Town, Ray Harrison from Boston United and winger Jackie Chew from Blackburn Rovers. This football season for Burnley (now back to the claret and blue strip) was to become one of the most successful in the clubs history with a sound defence and the goalscoring ability of Jack Billingham and Harry Potts. Burnley Football Club achieved promotion as runners-up to Manchester City and were FA Cup runners-up at Wembley against Charlton Athletic.

63

Jimmy Strong

1946 - 1952

Ron Brown

Goalkeeper Jimmy Strong was to set four separate goalkeeping records that season, conceding only 32 goals out of a total of fifty-one senior appearances, and on two occasions not conceding a league goal for 675 minutes as well as recording a total of 680 minutes in all competitions (League and Cup) with twenty-five clean sheets.

Burnley started the 1947–48 First Division campaign in fine form, with an eventual finish in third place.

Up until the 1948–49 season Jimmy Strong's consecutive appearances in League and FA Cup now stood at one hundred and thirty-nine with Burnley finishing in mid-table under new manager Frank Hill, who replaced Cliff Britton (who went on to manage Everton) just after the start of that season.

Up until the end of the 1949–50 season Jimmy Strong's consecutive appearances in the four seasons now stood at a record one hundred and eighty-four, with only 176 goals conceded, and a total of seventy-five clean sheets. Under Frank Hill's leadership, Burnley were to finish mid-table over these three seasons. During March, Jimmy Strong played in a record breaking number of consecutive matches, with a total of two hundred and three Football League consecutive appearances plus seventeen FA Cup appearances, making in all competitions a total of two hundred and twenty.

On 23 March 1951 in a First Division fixture at Turf Moor against Chelsea, Jimmy Strong was injured in a clash with forward Bobby Smith and was to miss the following two league matches with Joe McNulty deputising.

Jimmy Strong represented Burnley for the following two seasons up until 13 December 1952, when he made his last appearance for the club against Arsenal at Turf Moor in a 1–1 drawn game. With the purchase of goalkeeper Des Thompson from York City there was no way back, and at the end of May 1954 at the age of 37 he retired to run a poultry farm near his home in Burnley.

Jimmy Strong set many records at Burnley Football Club that will probably never be broken. He was no doubt one of the finest goalkeepers who ever played for Burnley Football Club.

DES THOMPSON
1952–54

Football League Appearances. 62

FA Cup Appearances 7

Total Goals Conceded 99

Total Clean Sheets 15

Average Conceded per Game 1.43

Desmond 'Des' Thompson was born 4 December 1928 in Southampton. His father had also been a goalkeeper who played for Southampton as was his brother George, who played for various clubs including Preston North End, played in the Cup Final of 1954.

His early career took him to Scunthorpe United, Gainsborough Trinity and Dinnington FC before signing professional for York City in January 1951. He was to make eighty Football League appearances for the Third Division North side before attracting the interest of Burnley Football Club, who were seeking a future replacement for their goalkeeping legend Jimmy Strong. A £7,350 offer was put in place and was accepted by York City in the November of 1952. Within a month of signing Des Thompson was selected for the First Division fixture at Middlesbrough on 20 December. In that side was future Scottish International John Aird and Burnley legend Harold Mather at full-backs. Jimmy Adamson, Tommy Cummings and Reg Attwell made up the half-back line-up. The two wingers were Jackie Chew and Billy Elliott, with Jimmy McIlroy, Bill Holden and Les Shannon making up the forward line. The game ended in a 2–2 draw, with goals for Burnley scored by Bill Holden and Billy Elliott.

With Jimmy Strong now demoted to reserve football, Des Thompson was now first choice goalkeeping selection for the remainder of this 1952–53 football season. He made a total of twenty-six Football League and FA Cup appearances,

Des Thompson
1952 - 1954

Ron Brown

recording a total of eight clean sheets, with Burnley Football Club finishing in a sixth position – their best since 1948.

The Burnley side at the start of the 1953–54 season, under manager Frank Hill, were now serious challengers for the First Division top spot, with new right-winger Billy Gray purchased from Chelsea making his debut. Goalkeeper Des

Thompson was now firm choice for selection and made a total of forty senior appearances that season. This included the FA Cup Third Round thriller at Turf Moor with Burnley entertaining Manchester United, where four goals were scored in the first seven minutes, with Burnley the final victors in this epic Cup tie which ended 5–3 to the home side. Des kept his position up until the April of this season and was rested after the home defeat by Chelsea.

Colin McDonald, who had initially signed for Burnley in 1948, made his debut in the next First Division fixture at Aston Villa, which ended in a 5–1 defeat for Burnley. Although this was a setback for Colin McDonald, was also selected for the final four First Division fixtures.

Burnley who finished in seventh place appointed a new manager who was no stranger to the club. For the commencement of the 1954–55 season Alan Brown, a solid half-back who made eighty-eight Football League appearances for Burnley at the recommencement of football after the hostilities of the Second World War, was put into the hot seat. Des Thompson was no longer first choice 'keeper with Colin McDonald now installed as first choice selection. Thompson made a further final three League appearances for Burnley, with his last game in a First Division fixture at Turf Moor on 27 November 1954 against Tottenham Hotspur, which ended in a 2–1 defeat. At the conclusion of that season, Des Thompson was transfer listed and signed for First Division rivals Sheffield United in May 1955.

Although he made 25 first team appearances for The Blades, it could not prevent them being relegated back to the Second Division at the end of the 1955–56 football season. He stayed at Sheffield United for a number of years involved in other footballing projects before eventually retiring from football in 1964. He died in 2010.

COLIN MCDONALD
1954–59

Football league Appearances 186

FA Cup Appearances 15

Total Goals Conceded 272

Total Clean Sheets 52

Average Conceded per Game .1.35

Honours:

England Caps 8

Goals Conceded 11

Colin Agnew McDonald was born on 15 October 1930 in Tottington, Bury, Lancashire. His father was a former goalkeeper who played for Bury and Portsmouth. In his schoolboy days, Colin McDonald played outside-left for his local Sunday School side Hawkshaw St Mary and would play in the goalkeeping position when required.

He was spotted by former Burnley full-back, Jack Marshall, who in 1948 arranged for Colin to have a trial at Burnley. He signed amateur terms for the club enabling him to play part-time football whilst still in employment as an apprentice plumber. He was loaned out to non-league side Headington United in 1950, where he made thirty appearances for them before returning to Burnley where he now played reserve team football. Colin McDonald was to become one of Burnley Football Clubs finest goalkeepers, with a six foot frame and a safe pair of hands, he made goalkeeping look easy.

On 10 April 1954 in a First Division fixture at Aston Villa, manager Frank Hill decided to give Colin his debut after resting first choice goalkeeper Des Thompson. In this Burnley side were the two Scottish full-backs, John Aird and Doug Winton. Jimmy Adamson, Eric Binns and Bobby Seith made up the half-

Colin in training before the main event

back line-up. On the wings were Billy Gray and Brian Pilkington, with the inside-forward line-up consisting of Jimmy McIlroy, Billy Holden and Les Shannon. It was a disastrous start to a promising career for Colin, with the game ending in a 5–1 defeat. Manager Frank Hill, unperturbed by Colin McDonald's performance, selected him for the remaining four Football League games with Colin keeping one clean sheet and conceding a respectable four goals.

With Burnley's new manager Alan Brown firmly in place for the commencement of the 1954–55 football season, no changes were made for the first home game against Cardiff City with Colin McDonald installed as first choice goalkeeper. After sixteen consecutive appearances for Burnley, Colin was rested after conceding five goals at Wolverhampton Wanderers, with Des Thompson taking over for the next three Football League games. Colin McDonald returned for Burnley and made the position his own with a total of 40 senior appearances, securing a mid-table tenth position finish for the club.

The 1955–56 season, with no opposition to his first choice goalkeeping selection, Colin McDonald made a total of forty-eight consecutive appearances for Burnley. This included the epic FA Cup fourth round encounter with Chelsea which went to five games (540 minutes) to decide who would progress to round five, with Burnley losing the final tie at White Hart Lane 2–0. It was a good season to be had, with Burnley finishing in seventh position.

Once again in command for the commencement of the 1956–57 season, Colin McDonald was selected for the first twenty-two Football League matches, but suffered an injury to his ankle at Chelsea. The subsequent eight Football League fixtures and five FA Cup ties were represented in the goalkeeping position by a young reserve team footballer Adam Blacklaw, who did enough to justify a career as a future first choice selection. Colin returned from injury for the Football League fixture on 9 March 1957 at Turf Moor against Sunderland and played the final twelve games of that campaign, with Burnley finishing in seventh position, the same as the previous season.

The 1957–58 football season for Colin McDonald was to be the pinnacle of his goalkeeping career. Under new manager Billy Dougall, who had replaced Alan Brown who departed for the managerial hot seat at Sunderland, no changes were made to the side with Colin McDonald firmly in place between the sticks. He was to make a total of forty-two senior appearances for Burnley that season, which saw another managerial change in the January with Harry Potts replacing Billy Dougall, who had to retire on health grounds. Burnley Football Club finished

Colin McDonald making a save at Bolton

that Football League season one better than the previous campaign with a sixth position finish.

On 18 May 1958 Colin McDonald was selected for England in a friendly in Moscow against the USSR, making him the third Burnley goalkeeper to represent England, which ended in a 1–1 drawn match. The World Cup in Sweden in June of that year saw Colin McDonald installed in the four World Cup games with a superb performance throughout. Another three international appearances would then follow in the autumn of 1958.

With the 1958–59 season now underway, with Colin being rested and Adam Blacklaw filling in the goalkeeping roll whilst on international duty, he returned and made the goalkeeping position on 14 March 1959 in a Football League fixture at Turf Moor against West Ham United. This, unknowing to everybody, would be his last for Burnley Football Club. He was selected to play for the Football League against the League of Ireland three days later and suffered a career finishing broken leg, which sidelined him for the remainder of the season.

The following season after recovery from these injuries, Colin played reserve football for Burnley, but could not retain the skills he possessed prior to that serious injury. He left Burnley for non-league Altrincham and later became chief scout at Bury. This was followed by administration work with Bolton Wanderers and Tranmere Rovers, before finally retiring from football. Had he not succumbed to those injuries would he have been selected for the 1962 and possibly the 1966 World Cup winning side? We will never know.

Colin McDonald, who in fact donated his first England cap to Burnley Football Club, was arguably one of Burnley's greatest goalkeepers, if not the greatest of them all.

ADAM BLACKLAW
1956–66

Football League Appearances. 318

FA Cup Appearances 44

European Cup Appearances 4

Inter Cities Fairs Cup Appearances 4

Football League Cup Appearances. 12

Football Association Charity Shield 1

Total Goals Conceded 570

Total Clean Sheets 92

Average Conceded per Game 1.49

Honours:

Football League Championship Medal 1959–60

Football League Runners Up Medal 1961–62

FA Cup Runners Up Medal   1961–62

International Caps (Scotland) 3

Goals Conceded 13

Adam Smith Blacklaw was born on 2 September 1937 in Aberdeen, Scotland. In his early schoolboy footballing days he played as a centre-forward and decided that goalkeeping was better suited for him. He was also a keen schoolboy boxer, and developed into a 6ft tall 15st frame, well suited for a future goalkeeper. He came to prominence in his early senior schoolboy days and played well enough to be selected for Scotland. Aberdeen Football Club were well aware of Adams talent and was interested in signing his as a youth.

Burnley, in their usual pursuit of players especially in the north of the British Isles, spotted Adam Blacklaw's ability in his goalkeeping position, enough to offer him a complete package deal. This consisted of an apprenticeship as a bricklayer

plus professional football terms, which he duly signed for Burnley Football Club in the October of 1954. Before he became understudy to first choice keeper Colin McDonald, he played his early football at junior level and reserve team football.

When Colin McDonald was injured at Chelsea in the December of 1956, Adam Blacklaw was offered his senior goalkeeping debut for the First Division fixture at Turf Moor on 22 December 1956 against Cardiff City. In that side that day was full-backs John Angus and Dougie Winton, with the half-back line-up of Bobby Seith, Jimmy Adamson and Brian Miller. On the wings were Dougie Newlands and Brian Pilkington, with the forward line consisting of Jimmy McIlroy, Les

75

Shannon and Albert Cheesebrough. Cardiff City opened the scoring in the sixth minute, which may have slightly dented Adam Blacklaw's appetite, but the outcome was a 6–2 victory for Burnley.

He was to remain in the first choice position for a further seven Football League fixtures and five FA Cup appearances, conceding a total of 14 goals and keeping four clean sheets, until the return from injury of Colin McDonald.

The following 1957–58 football season he played in the Central League for the reserves but for three Football League fixtures (whilst Colin was recalled for International duties) which included the 6–1 hammering at Chelsea on 21 September 1957. When Colin McDonald was seriously injured whilst playing for the Football League against the League of Ireland in the March of 1959, Adam Blacklaw took over his first team duties for the remainder of that 1958–59 campaign making it a total of fifteen Football League appearances.

With Colin McDonald unable to fulfil his first team duties for the commencement of the Football League Championship season of 1959–60, Adam Blacklaw was firmly installed as first choice 'keeper in manager Harry Potts side, missing just one fixture in that triumphant season.

With European Football beckoning the following season, Adam Blacklaw was at the pinnacle of his career, making a total for the 1960–61 season of sixty senior appearances, which included the four European Cup ties against Reims of France and SV Hamburg of Germany to whom they eventually lost out. Burnley also lost to Tottenham Hotspur in the semi-final of the FA Cup and also to Aston Villa in the semi-final of the Football League Cup, ending with a fourth place finish in the Football League.

The 1961–62 football season for Burnley could have been their greatest season in the history of the club. Burnley, who had been top of the Football League most of that season, went to previous promotion champions Ipswich Town at Portman Road on 29 August 1961, but it came as a shock to most clubs when Alf Ramsey adapted his side to play without wingers. Burnley came away from Ipswich that evening with Adam Blacklaw picking the ball out of the Burnley net six times in a 6–2 defeat. Ipswich, who eventually finished the season as Football League Champions, could have finished as runners-up had the result of that game been reversed with Burnley taking the title that season.

A Cup Final appearance at Wembley against Tottenham Hotspur was to follow, with Burnley once again finishing runners-up beaten by three goals to one.

Adam Blacklaw was to become first choice 'keeper over the next few Football League seasons with Scottish goalkeeper Harry Thomson installed as back up 'keeper. He was selected for his native Scotland in the January of 1963 in an International against Norway, which was to end in a 4–3 defeat. This was followed by two more International recalls, the last being in December of 1965 against Italy in Naples which ended in a 7–0 defeat for Scotland.

With Adam Blacklaw injured at Elland Road, Leeds in the March of 1965, it meant Adam would miss the final eight Football League fixtures that season with Harry Thomson deputising. When Adam Blacklaw came back from injury he was recalled for Burnley in the away fixture on 30 October 1965 against, of all teams, Leeds United at Elland Road.

Burnley Football Club, who finished the 1965–66 Football League season in third place, qualified for the Inter-Cities Fairs Cup for the following season. Adam Blacklaw was selected for the first four Cup ties of that competition, but was dropped for the final four ties in favour of Harry Thomson. He was to make his final Football League appearance at Stoke City on 27 December 1966 to make way for Harry Thomson who was firmly installed as first choice Burnley 'keeper.

He was transferred to Blackburn Rovers in the July of 1967 and made a total of ninety-six Football League appearances for them. He had later spells at Blackpool and Northern Premier League side Great Harwood, before turning to management with Clitheroe Town.

After retirement from football he went on to run a newsagents in Burnley and also had a spell as a pub landlord. He died on 28 February 2010.

HARRY THOMSON
1965–1969

Football League Appearances. 117

FA Cup Appearances 5

Football League Cup Appearances. 15

Inter Cities Fairs Cup Appearances 4

Total Goals Conceded 221

Total Clean Sheets 38

Average Conceded per Game 1.57

Harry Watson Thomson was born in Edinburgh on 25 August 1940. Upon leaving school he worked in the local mining industry. His early goalkeeping career started at Edinburgh District League junior side, Bo'ness United. He was short in height, 5ft 9in tall, which did not hamper his goalkeeping ability.

Burnley scouts, in their usual fishing pursuits of players from north of the border, which had brought success to the club in the past with players like Andy Lochhead, Adam Blacklaw and Dougie Winton, were attracted by Harry Thomson's goalkeeping talent. He was offered professional terms with Burnley Football Club playing junior and reserve football, and signed in the August of 1959. He was to become part of the successful reserve side that won the Central League in 1962 and the following 1963 season.

He became understudy to fellow Scot Adam Blacklaw, but due to Adam's injury in a league fixture at Leeds United in the March of 1965, Harry Thomson was called upon to fill his role in the following Football League fixture at Leicester City on 20 March 1965. He made his goalkeeping debut for Burnley, which they won 2–0, with Harry Thomson saving a penalty. In that side were full-backs Sammy Todd and Alex Elder. The half-back line consisted of Brian O'Neil, John Talbut and Brian Miller. The two wingers were Willie Morgan and Ralph Coates

with Andy Lochhead, Willie Irvine and Arthur Bellamy making up the forward line-up. Harry Thomson was to remain in the number one spot for the remaining eight Football League fixtures of this 1964–65 season, conceding eight goals and keeping three clean sheets.

He was to make the first thirteen Football League fixtures and two Football

League Cup ties of the 1965–66 football season, but with the return from injury of Adam Blacklaw, he was demoted back to reserve football. He made a couple of appearances for Burnley in the February of 1966 with the club finishing the season in a healthy third place position.

After once again being understudy to Adam Blacklaw for the commencement of the 1966–67 season, it was manager Harry Potts decision to drop Adam Blacklaw from the Burnley side and install Harry Thomson in his place as first choice goalkeeper. Potts selected him for the home Football League fixture against West Bromwich Albion, which ended in a 5–1 victory for Burnley. He kept his position for the remainder of that season which included four Inter-Cities Fairs Cup ties.

It was his historic performance in an away tie at Napoli in Italy on 8 February 1967 that will long be remembered. As well as saving a penalty it was his other attributes throughout this match that will never be forgotten. He was now christened 'The God in a Green Jersey'.

For the next two football seasons, Harry Thomson was Burnley's first choice goalkeeper with Rodney Jones deputising for nine of those Football League fixtures. Burnley were to finish in fourteenth position in both of these football seasons and on two occasions conceded eight goals at West Bromwich Albion in the November of 1967 and seven goals at Tottenham in the September of 1968.

Due to his belligerent attitude towards the management at Burnley Football Club at the end of the 1968–69 season, they decided to terminate Harry Thomson's contract with the club and place him on the transfer list. His last game for Burnley was at Turf Moor on 23 April 1969 in a Football League fixture against Sunderland, which ended in a 2–1 home defeat. He was transferred to Second Division Blackpool, helping them to promotion back to the First Division, where he made sixty-one appearances before moving to Barrow in 1971, where he made 40 appearances.

PETER MELLOR
1969–72

Peter Joseph Mellor was born on 20 November 1947 in Prestbury, Cheshire. He was offered a trial at Manchester United, but was subsequently turned down and joined neighbours Manchester City as an apprentice. He was capped whilst at City with the England youth side against Wales, which ended in a 4–1 victory in March 1966. Unable to progress further he joined non-league football club Witton Albion in 1967, where he stayed for two seasons.

Having attracted the attentions of Burnley Football Club, the tall, fair haired, ever smiling Peter Mellor was offered a trial at Burnley, he impressed enough to be offered professional terms, which he duly signing in May 1969.

Burnley, who had now dismissed first choice goalkeeper Harry Thomson, were somewhat short of a goalkeeper for the coming 1969–70 football season. Peter Mellor was thrust into Harry Potts opening Football League Division One fixture at Derby County on 9 August 1969. With Peter Mellor being the only debutant that day, the side were unchanged from the previous season with full-backs consisting of John Angus and Les Latcham. The half-back line-up were Brian O'Neil, Colin Waldron and Sammy Todd. On the wings were Dave Thomas and Steve Kindon, with the others Ralph Coates, Frank Casper and Mike Docherty making the forward line-up. The result ended in a goalless draw, with Peter Mellor sustaining a hand injury in the final few minutes and full-back Les Latcham taking over as a

substitute goalkeeper.

Throughout the remainder of that season Peter Mellor remained consistent, with fifty senior appearances to his credit and conceding a total of sixty-eight goals, with Burnley finishing in fourteenth position for the fourth season in succession

Burnley Football Club, at the commencement of the 1970–71 season had new manager Jimmy Adamson in place. They decided to bring in veteran ex-England goalkeeper Tony Waiters from Liverpool, as player coach and back up for keeper Peter Mellor. In a pre-season Football match Peter Mellor dislocated his shoulder and was unable to fulfil his obligations with Waiters being called up for the opening fixture against his previous club Liverpool. It was not until the November of 1970 that he was fit enough to be recalled for Burnley in the home fixture against Nottingham Forest

After five appearances for Burnley, Peter Mellor was dropped from the side until he was once again recalled for two Football League fixtures at the end of that campaign. Burnley were relegated with Blackpool at the end of this term, returning to the Second Division after a 24 year stay in the top division.

At the start of the 1971–72 season, Peter Mellor was recalled (after Tony Waiters was dropped after three Second Division appearances) for the away fixture at Preston, which ended in a 3–1 win for Jimmy Adamson's side. Peter Mellor was to make a further nineteen Football League appearances, his last game for Burnley being the home defeat by Huddersfield Town in the third round of

Peter Mellor making a save at Upton Park against West Ham United

the FA Cup, with the Clarets going down 1-0 to the visitors. With a deal to bring goalkeeper Alan Stevenson from Chesterfield, it was agreed to loan Peter Mellor in a exchange deal where he made four goalkeeping appearances. A month later Burnley agreed to Fulham's offer of £25,000 for the services of Peter Mellor, where he made one hundred and ninety league appearances for the Cottagers. He was to make an FA Cup Final appearance in 1975 for Fulham against West Ham United, losing to the Hammers 2–0, with both goals scored by a future Burnley forward Alan Taylor.

He joined Hereford United in 1977 making thirty-two senior appearances before moving the following season to Portsmouth, where he made a further one hundred and twenty-nine appearances.

In 1982 he moved to Canada and made a further twenty-seven appearances for Edmonton Drillers, then took up coaching where he went to live in The United States.

TONY WAITERS
1970–71

Football League Appearances. 38

FA Cup Appearances 1

Football League Cup Appearances. 1

Texaco Cup Appearances 2

Total Goals Conceded 66

Total Clean Sheets 9

Average Conceded per Game 1.57

Anthony Keith Waiters was born on 1 February 1937 in Southport, Merseyside. In 1957, at the age of 20, he began his goalkeeping career at amateur football club Bishop Auckland. He was transferred to non-league Macclesfield Town in 1958 and made eleven appearances for them. Whilst still at college in 1959 he was called upon to play for England at amateur level.

It was while he was there that he caught the eye of the then Blackpool manager Ron Suart, who needed a replacement for current goalkeeper George Farm. He signed for Blackpool on professional terms where he made a total of two hundred and fifty senior appearances for them in his eight year stay, up until the end of the 1966–67 football season. He was to represent England where he was capped five times and was back up to England goalkeeping legend Gordon Banks.

He initially retired from football in 1967 when his club Blackpool where relegated from the First Division and joined Liverpool's Youth Development Academy as coach. Harry Potts invited Tony Waiters to join the coaching staff at Turf Moor in 1970, as well as enticing him out of retirement as back up for first choice goalkeeper Peter Mellor.

With the occurrence of the shoulder injury that Peter sustained in the pre-

season of the 1970–71 campaign, Burnley were left without reasonable cover and Tony Waiters was the only option for the opening Football League Division One fixture at Turf Moor against his old club Liverpool on 15 August 1970. There were a few changes in this Burnley side, who lost this opener 2–1 with James Thomson at left-half, Geoff Nulty at centre-forward and at inside-left Doug Collins. Tony Waiters kept the goalkeeping position for the following sixteen Football League fixtures until the return from injury of Peter Mellor for the home fixture against Nottingham Forest on 21 November 1970.

Peter Mellor was dropped from the Burnley side after five appearances with the team struggling at the foot of the First Division in Jimmy Adamson's first full season in charge, with Tony Waiters recalled to the side. Tony made a total of thirty-nine senior appearances that season, conceding a total of sixty-one goals and keeping nine clean sheets. Burnley were relegated along with Tony's old club Blackpool, and both facing the prospects of Second Division Football for the forthcoming season.

Tony Waiters was selected for the first three Second Division fixtures of the 1971–72 season. His final game for Burnley was at Oxford United on 28 August 1971 where Burnley suffered a 2–1 defeat. With the return of Peter Mellor, it was now clear that retirement from playing football was possible and he terminated his contract with Burnley in 1972.

He took up management at Plymouth Argyle soon after leaving Burnley and led them to promotion as champions of the Third Division in 1975. After leaving

Plymouth Argyle in 1977 he moved to Canadian side Vancouver Whitecaps and finally became manager of the national side before finally retiring from football in 1991. He was probably the second Burnley goalkeeper who was enticed out of retirement, the previous being Ted Adams in 1936.

ALAN STEVENSON
1972–83

Football League Appearances. 438

FA Cup Appearances 33

Football League Cup Appearances. 36

Texaco Cup Appearances 7

Watney Cup Appearances. 2

FA Charity Shield Appearances. 1

Anglo Scottish Cup Appearances 19

Football League Trophy Appearances 4

Total Goals Conceded 717

Total Clean Sheets 151

Average Conceded Per Game. 1.33

Honours:

Second Division Championship Medal 1972–73

Third Division Championship Medal 1981–82

Anglo Scottish Cup Winning Medal 1978–79

Alan Stevenson was born on 6 November 1950 in Staveley, Derbyshire and was to become a cult figure at Burnley Football Club alongside previous goalkeeping legends from the past. In his younger junior footballing days he was rejected by other clubs, including Burnley, eventually signing for Fourth Division Chesterfield as an amateur. As well as playing football he was also a talented cricketer having had trials for Derbyshire County Cricket Club, which made Alan a good all-rounder.

In 1969 he was offered full professional terms with Chesterfield and was a member of the clubs successful 1969–70 Fourth Division Championship winning side. By 1972 Alan had made one hundred and four league appearances for the

Spirites and was attracting the attentions of other Football League clubs that included Derby County and Leeds United, with Burnley also an interested party. With only goalkeeper Jeff Parton on Burnley's books in January 1972, Jimmy Adamson had to move fast to secure Alan Stevenson's signature. Adamson and three members of staff made an appointment to meet Alan with his Chesterfield representatives at the Woodall service station, situated on the M1 motorway. The deal was completed with Chesterfield receiving £50,000 and the loan of Peter Mellor, who would eventually sign for Fulham for £25,000.

Alan Stevenson, now a Burnley player, made his Football League Division Two debut at Brisbane Road against Orient on 22 January 1972 in a 1–0 defeat for Burnley. In his side that day was full-backs Mike Docherty and Jim Thomson. The half-back line consisted of Alan West, Colin Waldron and Martin Dobson. The wingers were Dave Thomas and Leighton James, with forwards Frank Casper, Paul Fletcher and Steve Kindon completing the line-up.

Alan Stevenson made a total of seventeen Football League appearances in this first season, conceding 22 goals and five clean sheets, and at one period did not concede a goal in 432 minutes of football. Burnley could only manage a seventh place finish in this first season back in the Second Division, but all hopes were on a successful 1972–73 campaign.

Burnley made an immediate impact in the second season back in the second tier of English football; more or less topped the division throughout with the Second Division Championship won in their final fixture at Preston North End. Alan Stevenson made forty-two consecutive Football League appearances that season, conceding only 35 goals with eighteen clean sheets and did not concede a goal in 510 minutes of football from 31 March 1973 till 28 April 1973. In this same season he was selected for the England Under 23's, for the first of his eleven caps, against Wales in the November of 1972

Jimmy Adamson's team of the seventies certainly lived up to its name with a sixth place finish in their 1973–74 return to the First Division, with Alan Stevenson missing only two league fixtures that season.

With a tenth place finish the following 1974–75 football season, Alan Stevenson missed only three league fixtures, as well as establishing Burnley Football Club as a well drilled First Division outfit.

The 1975–76 season started well with the signing of Mike Summerbee from Manchester City, but Burnley spent the rest of this campaign on the slide, with goalkeeper Alan Stevenson conceding four goals in a home fixture against Norwich City, followed by another five at home to Wolverhampton Wanderers. He was subsequently dropped from the side to be replaced by reserve goalkeeper Gerry Peyton, who was purchased as understudy to Alan. With Burnley hovering at the foot of the First Division table throughout, Jimmy Adamson resigned as manager to be replaced by Joe Brown in the January of 1976. This did not prevent the inevitable happening, with Burnley relegated back to the Second Division after a three-season stay.

With Alan Stevenson now playing reserve football for the commencement of the 1976–77 league campaign, it did not take long for him to win back selection with the transfer of Gerry Peyton to Football League side Fulham and also the return of former Burnley manager Harry Potts.

Alan Stevenson was to play in 127 consecutive matches up till the October of the 1979–80 football season, but this could not prevent the inevitable happening. With Brian Miller installed as manager in place of Harry Potts, Burnley struggled throughout that season and were finally relegated, with Charlton Athletic, into the third tier of English football for the first time in the clubs history.

With Burnley now a third division outfit for the 1980–81 football season, Alan Stevenson was to break certain records. From 30 August 1980 to 7 October 1980 he didn't concede a Football League goal, totaling 675 minutes, equaling Jimmy Strong's 1946 achievement.

It took the club two seasons to win promotion back to the second division under Brian Miller's managership, but the rot set in the following 1982–83 season. This could not prevent Burnley, for a second time, avoiding relegation back to the third tier, with Frank Casper at the helm since the middle of that term. Alan Stevenson made a total of forty-six senior appearances that season, which included the League Cup semi-final, losing to Liverpool on aggregate. It was to become his final season at Burnley, with the last fixture of the season at Derby County on 30 April 1983 ending in a 2–0 defeat.

Stevenson was just one appearance short of Jimmy McIlroy's 439 Football League appearances and was the second longest serving goalkeeper to play for Burnley.

In the August of 1983 he signed for Rotherham United where he made twenty-four appearances, followed by a spell at Hartlepool United, before finally retiring as a player. He became Commercial Manager for several football clubs, including York City where he is currently involved.

GERRY PEYTON
1975–1976

Football League Appearances. 30

FA Cup Appearances 1

Football League Cup Appearances. 1

Anglo Scottish Cup Appearances 2

Total Goals Conceded 48

Total Clean Sheets 10

Average Conceded per Game 1.41

Gerald Joseph Peyton was born in Birmingham on 20 May 1956 and his goalkeeping career spanned over thirty years, which included his involvement in coaching for various football clubs. In his early career he was rejected by several Football League clubs, but eventually signed for non-league Atherstone Town.

Such was his agility and safe handling that Atherstone Town manager, Gil Merrick, the former England and Birmingham City goalkeeper, recommended him to Burnley Football Club. A fee of £10,000 was agreed for the services of Gerry Peyton in the May of 1975, initially purchased as back up to Burnley keeper Alan Stevenson.

In the December of the 1975–76 season, with Burnley struggling at the foot of the First Division table, manager Jimmy Adamson decided to rest Alan Stevenson and give Gerry Peyton his Football League goalkeeping debut for the club. On 6 December 1975 Burnley faced Liverpool, who eventually won the division, at Turf Moor in a First Division fixture. Gerry Peyton took his place in the side, which included full backs Mike Docherty and Keith Newton. The half-back line-up consisted of Bill Ingham, Colin Waldron and Jim Thomson, on the wings were Mike Summerbee and Paul Bradshaw. Completing the forward line-up were Kevin Kennerley, Ray Hankin and Brian Flynn. The outcome ended in a 0–0 draw to give Gerry Peyton a clean sheet in the first of his appearances for Burnley. Gerry Peyton was to make a further twenty senior appearances that season, which saw Joe Brown replace Jimmy Adamson as manager.

The most he conceded was four in the away defeat at Stoke City and conceded only 28 goals in the entire campaign with a total of six clean sheets. Burnley were relegated at the end of this term with Sheffield United after a three season stay in the top division.

At the commencement of the 1976–77 football season, Burnley entered into the newly formed Anglo Scottish Cup and Gerry was selected for the first of these

ties at Blackburn Rovers and finally a home tie against Bolton Wanderers. Gerry Peyton was selected for the first away Second Division fixture at Wolverhampton Wanderers and made a further nine Football League appearances, his final game for Burnley at Nottingham Forest on 23 October 1976, before finally being dropped from the side.

In December 1976 Fulham Football Club offered Burnley £35,000 for the services of Gerry Peyton, who would replace ex Burnley 'keeper Peter Mellor. Fulham Football Club certainly benefited from the purchase of Gerry Peyton, who gave them excellent service in a nine-season spell, making 345 league appearances for the Cottagers.

Between 1977 and 1992 he was capped for the Republic of Ireland thirty-three times and during this period he played for AFC Bournemouth and Everton whilst also being loaned out to several other Football League clubs. These included Bolton Wanderers, Norwich City, Brentford and Chelsea. Between 1993 and 1994 he had spells with Brentford and West Ham.

His playing career spanned 20 years, making a total of over 650 senior appearances for several Football League clubs. Since his goalkeeping retirement in 1994 he has gone into coaching for various clubs and is presently goalkeeping coach at Arsenal Football Club.

The final question is, what if Burnley had held onto a goalkeeper of Gerry Peyton's talent and not sold him on to Fulham (where he made over 345 Football League appearances) as well as being awarded 33 International caps for Northern Ireland. He could have been immortal in the history of Burnley Football Club and many believe he was 'the one that got away'.

ROGER HANSBURY
1983–85

Roger Hansbury was born on 26 January 1955 in Barnsley, Yorkshire. He started his goalkeeping career at Norwich City in 1973, where he made seventy-eight Football League appearances in a seven season spell. During his time there he was loaned to various Football League clubs that included Bolton Wanderers, Cambridge United and Orient. Unable to gain first team selection at Norwich City, he moved to Hong Kong football side Eastern Athletic on a two-year deal.

At the commencement of the 1983–84 season Burnley, who had been relegated the previous season, installed John Bond as manager. He had had previous spells at Manchester City, AFC Bournemouth and Norwich City. John Bond, in his revolution that he promised for Burnley Football Club, brought in a lot of new playing staff from his former clubs. For the opening Third Division away fixture at Hull City on 27 August 1983, they saw four changes to the side with Roger Hansbury returning from Hong Kong to make his goalkeeping debut. In this side was a promising right-back, Lee Dixon, with left-back Willie Donachie partnering him. The half-back line-up were Mike Phelan, new signing Joe Callagher and Brian Flynn. The two wingers were Derek Scott and another new signing Thomas Hutchison. Making the forward line-up were final new signing Kevin Reeves with Billy Hamilton and Kevin Young. The final result ended with

a 4–1 defeat at the hands of Hull City.

Throughout this campaign Burnley were showing some promise, but were to finally finish mid-table in twelfth position. Roger Hansbury made a total of fifty-seven consecutive goalkeeping appearances, conceding 77 goals with fifteen clean sheets.

With the resignation of manager John Bond at the seasons end, his assistant John Benson took over the reins for the commencement of the coming 1984–85 Football League season. Roger Hansbury was once again first choice 'keeper for the opening Third Division home fixture against Plymouth Argyle. In the League Cup, in a two-legged tie in the October of that season, Roger Hansbury conceded a total of seven goals against Manchester United. After twenty-three league starts, with Burnley now in a perilous twentieth league position and facing relegation, Roger was dropped to be replaced by Joe Neenan. After missing nine Football League fixtures Roger was reinstated to the side against AFC Bournemouth on 23 March 1985 and kept his place for the remainder of that campaign. This ended with relegation to the Fourth Division of the Football League for Burnley Football Club for the first time in the clubs history.

His final appearance for Burnley was on 11 May 1985 at Walsall where Burnley secured a 3–2 victory. He was transfer listed and signed for Cambridge United soon after, where he made thirty-seven league appearances in his only season there. The following season he signed for Birmingham City, once again for John Bond, where he stayed for a three seasons spell, as well as being loaned to various clubs. These included Sheffield United, Wolverhampton Wanderers and Colchester United.

Finally, in 1989 he signed for Cardiff City where he played ninety-nine league games in a three season spell before retiring to run a greetings card shop.

JOE NEENAN
1985–87

Football League Appearances. 90

FA Cup Appearances 3

Football League Cup Appearances. 4

Football League Trophy Appearances 7

Total Goals Conceded 156

Total Clean Sheets 21

Average Conceded per Game 1.50

Joseph Patrick Neenan was born on 17 March 1959 in Manchester. He started his goalkeeping career at York City in 1976 where he made a total of fifty-six Football League appearances in his four-year stay, before being transferred to Scunthorpe United in 1980. In a five year career there he made a total of 191 senior goalkeeping appearances and was loaned out to Burnley in January 1985 for a two month period, where he made a total of nine Football League appearances and two Football League Trophy appearances.

His debut for Burnley was in the Football League Trophy first round, first leg tie on the 29 January 1985 against Stockport County at Turf Moor, which ended in a 5–1 victory for Burnley. In the side that day were full-backs Geoff Palmer and Peter Hampton. At half-back were Mike Phelan, Vince Overson and Kevin Hird. The wingers were Neil Grewcock and Tom Hutchison, with Stephen Kennedy, Peter Devine and Wayne Biggins completing the forward line-up.

The following Saturday on 2 February, Burnley convincingly beat Rotherham United 7–0 to complete a 12 goal spree in the two games in which goalkeeper Joe Neenan was involved. In the March of this season he returned to Scunthorpe United until the end of the 1984–85 campaign. Here, he was

known to be a good friend of cricket legend Ian Botham, who was in fact was playing for Scunthorpe United at the time.

At the commencement of the 1985–86 campaign, with Burnley now in the fourth tier of English football for the first time in their history they decided to bid for Joe Neenan's signature, as the goalkeeping position at Burnley became vacant due to the transfer of Roger Hansbury to Cambridge United. Joe Neenan, now installed as first choice 'keeper played in the opening fixture at Turf Moor on 17 August 1985 against Northampton Town with new manager and ex Manchester United player Martin Buchan in the manager's hot seat. He played in the first eight games of this season, but was dropped from the side to be replaced by Dennis Peacock, who himself made a total of eight appearances. Joe Neenan was recalled for the home fixture against Exeter City at the end of October, with another manager in place – Tommy Cavanagh – who was the previous manager Martin Buchan's trainer. Joe Neenan was now first choice keeper to the end of this 1985–86 season and made a total of forty-two senior appearances.

Burnley Football Club decided to reinstate Burnley legend Brian Miller into the management hot seat for the second time, for the season that will long be remembered in the clubs history (Joe's fourth manager). Burnley were struggling throughout this campaign with the second half of the season in the bottom four. Joe was to play throughout that season, but for one game on 24 January 1987 against Hereford United in a home Fourth Division fixture. It must have been a nightmare scenario for reserve keeper Anthony Woodworth, who was to concede six goals in his only appearance for Burnley, where the defence were also to blame for this post war record home defeat.

The season will long be remembered for the final Football League home fixture against Orient on 9 May 1987, where without a win Burnley would have been relegated (as bottom club) from the Football League, but for the two goal heroes, Ian Britton and Neil Grewcock who gave Burnley a 2–1 home win and security for the football club. This, like several players who represented Burnley that day, was Joe Neenan's last appearance for the club and he was transfer listed and signed for Peterborough United where he made a total of fifty-five Football League appearances. After a brief spell at Scarborough he finally retired from football.

CHRIS PEARCE
1987–92

Football League Appearances. 181

FA Cup Appearances 15

Football League Cup Appearances. 16

Football League Play-off Appearances.   2

Football League Trophy Appearances 18

Total Goals Conceded 280

Total Clean Sheets 74

Average Conceded per Game 1.21

Honours:

Fourth Division Championship Medal. 1991–92

Football League Trophy Runners Up Medal 1987–88

Christopher Leslie Pearce was born in Newport, Wales on 7 August 1961. In his early footballing career he was a goalkeeping apprentice at Wolverhampton Wanderers, but was deemed unsuitable for professional terms with the club.

In 1979, at the age of eighteen, he was offered professional terms at Blackburn Rovers whose manager at that time was Howard Kendall. Still unable to gain first team football he was loaned out to Rochdale and Barnsley, before being transferred permanently to Fourth Division Rochdale on a free transfer, where he made thirty-six appearances in the 1982–83 football season.

For the following three seasons he signed for Port Vale making a further forty-eight appearances. He was involved in Vales Fourth Division promotion success in the 1985–86 campaign, but eventually lost his position there.

Chris Pearce was becoming a much travelled journeyman and after Port

Vale gave him a free transfer he joined Fourth Division Wrexham for the 1986–87 season, making twenty-five goalkeeping appearances as well as an European Cup Winners Cup appearance against Real Zaragoza of Spain.

Brian Miller who at the start of the 1987–88 football season at Burnley made several changes to the playing squad including the £4,000 purchase from Wrexham of goalkeeper Chris Pearce. For the visit of Colchester United on 15 August 1987 at Turf Moor Burnley made seven changes in the starting line-up for this league match. Making their football debuts for Burnley that afternoon was goalkeeper Chris Pearce and at left-back Shaun McGrory, and the half-back newcomers were Peter Daniel and Peter Zelem. The three inside-forwards also making their debuts were Andy Farrell, George Oghani and Paul Comstive. The two wingers were the goal scoring heroes of the previous season, Neil Grewcock and Ian Britton. The game ended in a 3–0 defeat.

The season was to see a change in fortune for Burnley Football Club and goalkeeper Chris Pearce, in his first season, was to make a total of fifty-nine first senior appearances. This included a day out at Wembley for Burnley, where they met Wolverhampton Wanderers in the Final of the Football League Trophy on 29 May 1988. Although they were beaten by the Fourth Division champions 2–0 this was a complete contrast to the previous season with a tenth position finish in the league.

The following 1988–89 football season, Chris Pearce was to make a total of thirty-nine Football League appearances, missing the seven of the final league fixtures due to a facial injury with David Williams taking over until the final game when Pearce returned. In the January of this season, Frank Casper replaced Brian Miller for a second time with Burnley once again finishing in the bottom half of the division in sixteenth place.

The 1989–90 season was much the same, with Burnley going nowhere and finishing once again in sixteenth position, with Chris Pearce making a total of forty-nine senior appearances.

Frank Casper's Burnley made vast improvements the following 1990–91 season with Chris making a total of fifty-five senior appearances, which included the Play-offs that Burnley qualified for as sixth place finishers. This was the first time since 1898, 93 years earlier, that Burnley were involved in a knock-out competition to secure promotion, when they were involved in the old test match competition. Promotion was not to be, as Torquay United overcome Burnley in this two-legged campaign, winning by a 2–1 aggregate.

In the October of the following 1991–92 season, Jimmy Mullen was installed as manager, replacing Frank Casper. Goalkeeper Chris Pearce's involvement that season was quite sparse making a total of twenty-two senior appearances, with a total of five goalkeepers used during the successful season with Burnley winning the Fourth Division of the Football League. His final game for Burnley was the home fixture on 20 April 1992 for the visit of Scarborough which ended in a 1–1 drawn match.

Chris Pearce was transfer listed soon after the end of this successful campaign and joined Bradford City of the new Second Division, where he made nine league appearances before moving into non-league football.

Chris Pearce was, in his six seasons at Burnley, a loyal servant to the club making 236 senior appearances for them and will always be remembered as such.

MARLON BERESFORD
1992–98 AND 2002–03

Football League Appearances. . . . . 286 (1 as sub)

FA Cup Appearances 25

Football League Cup Appearances. 22

Football League Trophy Appearances 13

Football League Play Off Appearances.   3

Total Goals Conceded 500

Total Clean Sheets 77

Average Conceded per Game 1.43

Marlon Beresford was born on 2 September 1969 in Lincoln, Lincolnshire and was to become a favourite with the Burnley fans over his three spells at the club.

He was like his predecessor Chris Pearce, a much travelled journeyman due to the loan systems that were now freely operational. In his early teens he joined Sheffield Wednesday in 1987 as a junior, and with the loan system in place he played for Bury, Northampton Town and Crewe Alexandra, with a total number of thirty-one appearances for these three football clubs.

Burnley Football Club, who won the Fourth Division in 1992, were short of a goalkeeper due to Chris Pearce's move to Bradford City and

with only goalkeeper David Williams available made an offer in the August 1992 of £95,000 for the signing of Marlon Beresford, which was accepted. Burnley manager Jimmy Mullen had no hesitation in giving Marlon his debut for the home fixture against visitors Rotherham United, in what was now a reformed Second Division, on 29 August 1992. The game ended in a 1–1 drawn game. With Marlon in goal the full-backs were Ian Measham and Joe Jakub, with Adrian Randall, John Pender and Mark Monington at half-backs. The two wingers were Rob Painter and Steven Harper with John Deary, Graham Lancashire and Adrian Heath completing the forward line-up.

In his first full season at Burnley Marlon Beresford made a total of fifty-one senior appearances, with the club finishing their first season, 1992–93, in the Second Division in a mid table thirteenth position.

The following 1993–94 campaign was to end in Wembley glory once again, with qualification to the Play-offs resulting from a sixth position finish and a 3–1 aggregate two-legged victory over Plymouth Argyle. Stockport County who were Burnley's opponents that day were soundly beaten 2–1, which promoted the club back to the second tier of English football with Marlon Beresford making fifty-nine consecutive goalkeeping appearances and keeping fourteen clean sheets.

The following 1994–95 football season for Burnley ended with relegation once more, with a twenty-first position in the table and Burnley more or less struggling throughout the season. Liverpool were Burnleys opponents in both the League Cup and FA Cup, the Clarets lost in both competitions and Liverpool went on to lift the Football League Cup that season.

In the following 1995–96 football season, Marlon Beresford was to play under three managers, with ex Burnley player Adrian Heath installed as manager late in the March of the campaign. Burnley finished the campaign in seventeenth place with Marlon rested for ten of these football fixtures and Wayne Russell standing in. From 25 February 1997 until 22 March 1997 Marlon Beresford played a total of 434 minutes without conceding, Burnley finished this season, under Adrian Heath, in a much improved ninth position.

106

Another ex Burnley player, Chris Waddle, was installed for the 1997–98 season and Marlon Beresford in his sixth season as first choice 'keeper, made forty-three senior appearances until the end of his first spell at Burnley Football Club before his transfer to Premier League side Middlesbrough.

In his time at Middlesbrough he made only ten appearances for them, before being loaned out to his old club Sheffield Wednesday and Wolverhampton Wanderers before being briefly loaned back to Burnley in January 2002, where he made thirteen Football League appearances.

After a brief loan spell at York City for the commencement of the 2002–03 season, he made six senior appearances. He was official signed back to Burnley by manager Stan Ternent soon after and made his first appearance in his third spell, at Derby County on 7 September 2002, which Burnley won 2–1. In this his last season at the club, who finished in sixteenth place, he made forty-two senior appearances and was put on as sub for the home fixture against Sheffield Wednesday on 26 April 2003 after first choice 'keeper Nik Michopoulos was injured whilst Burnley were 3–1 down at half–time. Marlon Beresford was to concede a further four second half goals in a 7–2 defeat.

His final game for Burnley was the away fixture at Wimbledon, which ended in a 2–1 defeat. After he left Burnley on a free transfer at the end of this campaign he played a further four seasons at Bradford City, Luton Town (twice) and Barnsley as well as a loan spell with Oldham Athletic.

Marlon Beresford, who in his eleven year on and off spell with Burnley made a total of 349 (1 sub) senior appearances and will always be remembered as one of the truly goalkeeping greats at Burnley, ranking along side former 'keepers Colin McDonald, Adam Blacklaw and Alan Stevenson.

PAUL CRICHTON
1998–2001

Football League Appearances. . . . . 82 (1 as sub)

FA Cup Appearances. 4

Football League Cup Appearances 4

Football League Trophy Appearances 2

Total Goals Conceded 120

Total Clean Sheets 30

Average Conceded per Game 1.30

Honours:

Second Division Runners up Medal 1999–2000

Paul Andrew Crichton was born in Pontefract, Yorkshire on 3 October 1968. In 1986, in his early youth career, he joined Nottingham Forest as a trainee goalkeeper turning professional soon after. Although he did not get the opportunity at Forest he was loaned out to six Football League clubs to gain further experience, they included Notts County, Darlington, Swindon Town, Rotherham United, Peterborough United, and Torquay United. In this two year loan spell he made over forty senior goalkeeping appearance before finally signing full-time at Peterborough United where he was to make forty-seven Football League appearances in his two year stay until 1990.

From 1990 until 1993 he played for Doncaster Rovers making seventy-seven Football League appearances, which included the saving of a three times taken penalty at Rochdale in September 1990. He was given a free transfer at the end of the 1992–93 season and signed for Third Division side Grimsby Town. During his three season stay there he made one hundred and thirty-three Football League appearances before finally signing (after a five game loan spell) for West Bromwich Albion in 1996, where he made a total of twenty-seven league appearances.

During this spell he was loaned to Aston Villa and Burnley. His first appearance for Burnley as a loanee was for the Football League Division Two opening game of the 1998–99 season at Turf Moor against Bristol Rovers, which ended in a 2–1 victory to the home side. Also playing in new manager Stan Ternents side were, defenders Chris Brass and Stephen Morgan. The midfielders were Mark Ford, Steven Blatherwick, Lee Howey and Glen Little. In the forward line-up were Mike Williams, Andy Cooke, Andy Payton and Paul Smith. Paul Crichton, who had only played the one game for Burnley, was targeted by Stan Ternent to replace first choice 'keeper Gavin Ward in the November (three months after his first game) of the season and an offer of £100,000 to West Bromwich Albion for goalkeeper Paul was duly accepted. He made his second debut for Burnley at AFC Bournemouth and conceded five goals in a 5–0 defeat. He made twenty-eight consecutive Football League appearances to the end of this first season, with the club finishing in fifteenth position.

The season will be long remembered for the visit of Gillingham on 27 February 1999 when their forward Bob Taylor scored five goals for the visitors (a post war record) and the following Saturday at Turf Moor Manchester City put six goals into Paul Crichton's net. In his first season for Burnley he conceded fifty goals with seven clean sheets.

It was all about to change in the following 1999–2000 campaign with many changes to the playing squad, which were orchestrated by manager Stan Ternent. Having been in the top five all season promotion was a possibility. This was achieved within the last two games of the season with a runners–up final position to Division Two champions Preston North End. Paul Crichton made a total of fifty-three consecutive senior appearances for Burnley that season, conceding 58 goals with twenty-one clean sheets.

After making seven appearances at the 2000–01 campaign Paul Crichton was dropped from the side in favour of new signing, Greek International Nikolaos Michopoulos, His last game for Burnley was as sub for Nik Michopoulos at his old club West Bromwich Albion, which ended with a 1–1 draw.

He was transfer listed at the end of this campaign and signed for Norwich City in a £150,000 deal that kept him there for three seasons. In his spell there he was on loan to several clubs before eventually signing for York City, where he was sacked after only four appearances.

With many other clubs to follow, including a one season stint at Accrington Stanley where he made nineteen appearances before moving to Cambridge United in 2006 and making a further thirty-two appearances, he finally made the position of player-coach which he would finally settle into when he retired from his playing career. His last coaching assignment was at Queens Park Rangers, which he left in January 2016.

NIK MICHOPOULOS
2000–03

Nikolaos Michopoulos was born on 20 February 1970 in Karditsa, Greece. In his early goalkeeping career he played for Greek Football Club Apouon Larissa, where he had a three-season spell between 1989 and 1992. In 1995 to 2000 he

played as a professional for Paok Salonika, making over one hundred and thirty senior appearances and in the process was honoured by his country Greece, winning thirteen caps in that five season spell.

With Burnley Football Club, under the managementship of Stan Ternent, now back in the second tier of English football signed three players from Greece in the August of 2000: goalkeepers Nik Michopoulos and Luigi Cennamo and centre-forward Dimitrios Papadopoulos.

Nik Michopoulos, made his goalkeeping debut for his club in the Football League Cup second round, first leg tie at Turf Moor on 19

Nik Michopoulos making a penalty save against Crystal Palace

September 2000 against opponents Crystal Palace. In the four-four-two line-up were defenders Ian Cox, Stephen Davis, Mitchell Thomas and Lee Briscoe. The midfielders were John Mullin, Kevin Ball, Paul Cook and Graham Branch, with Andy Cooke and Andy Payton making the forward line-up, with the outcome being a 2–2 drawn tie.

With first choice 'keeper Paul Crichton now dropped from the side, Nik made his Football League debut at Huddersfield Town four days later on 23 September 2000. He was to make a total of forty-three senior appearances to the end of this 2000–01 season, conceding 52 goals and keeping fifteen clean sheets with Burnley finishing just out of the play offs in seventh place.

For the commencement of the 2001–02 Football League season, Nik Michopoulos was first choice 'keeper for the opening game at Sheffield Wednesday and was firmly installed in that position for the next twenty-eight Football League fixtures.

In the fourth round FA Cup visit to Cheltenham on 26 January 2002 he was injured with the score at 0–0 with Luigi Cennamo taking over his goalkeeping position for the rest of this Cup-tie. Unable to continue for the following Football League fixtures, ex Burnley goalkeeper Marlon Beresford was drafted in for the

113

following thirteen league matches with Nik returning to fulfil the final five to this season. Burnley narrowly missed out on a play-off position on goal difference and once again finished in seventh place.

In the May of 2002 Nik was selected for Greece where he made two appearances as sub, bringing his total of International caps to fifteen.

After five appearances at the start of the 2002–03 Football League Division One season Nik Michopoulos was dropped after the home fixture against Crystal Palace on 31 August 2002, with Burnley now in bottom position with one point out of fifteen. With Marlon Beresford once again taking over the goalkeeping position, Nik (because of financial difficulties within the club) was loaned to Crystal Palace where he made a total of five Football League appearances before his return. He was reinstated for the home fixture on 11 January 2003 against Ipswich Town, followed by the FA Cup replay against Grimsby Town four days later. He was to make six more appearances for Burnley at the tail end of this season which saw Burnley close to relegation, finally finishing in nineteen position.

His final game was for the visit of Sheffield Wednesday on 26 April 2003 which ended in a 7–2 hammering from the Owls. With Nik injured with the score at 3–1 Marlon Beresford took over the remainder of this game where he conceded four more second half goals. In the June of 2003 Nik Michopoulos decided to retire from English football, moving back to his homeland Greece.

He was one of the first foreign goalkeeper to play for Burnley followed later by the arrivals of Brian Jenson from Denmark and Hungarian 'keeper Gábor Király.

BRIAN JENSEN
2003–2013

Football League Appearances. 229

Premier League Appearances 38

As Substitute (FL/PL) 4

FA Cup Appearances 17

Football League Cup Appearances. 19

Championship Play Off Appearances 3

Total Goals Conceded 416

Total Clean Sheets 91

Average Conceded per Game 1.36

Honours:

Championship Play Off Winners Medal 2008–09

Brian Paldan Jensen was born on 8 June 1975 near Copenhagen in Denmark and was to become a cult legend amongst the many Burnley fans and was baptised 'The Beast' in his early days at the club. Because of his 6ft 5in height he was perfectly suited for the goalkeeping position and would eventually play for Danish football clubs B93 and AZ Alkmaar, where he signed as a full time professional in 1998.

West Bromwich Albion who, like many clubs were scouting throughout Europe for future talent, took an interest in Brian Jensen and made an offer of £80,000 to AZ Alkmaar for his services and the deal was signed in March of 2000. In his three season spell with West Bromwich Albion he made a total of over forty-six senior appearances for the club, but with relegation from the Premier League that followed in 2003, Brian Jensen was subsequently transfer listed.

Burnley Football Club, with Stan Ternent in charge, took advantage of the situation and signed him for the forthcoming 2003–04 Football League season. He

made his goalkeeping debut for Burnley in the opening Football League game at Turf Moor against Crystal palace on 9 August 2003. Also making their debuts for Burnley that day were defenders Lee Roche and Mohamed Camara, who played alongside Graham Branch and Arthur Gnohere. In midfield, also making his debut, was Luke Chadwick who played alongside Paul Weller, Richard Chaplow and Glen Little, with Alan Moore and Robbie Blake making the forward line-up. The result ended in a 3–2 defeat for Burnley, but it cemented Brian Jensen's position within the club in his first season at Burnley, where he made a total of fifty-two consecutive senior appearances, with the outcome a nineteenth position finish just avoiding relegation by two points.

With the arrival of goalkeeper Danny Coyne, who signed from Leicester City in July 2004, Brian's future with Burnley as first choice 'keeper for the forthcoming

2004–05 football season was In doubt, with new club manager Steve Cotterill now firmly in control. Brian Jensen was recalled to the side at Queens Park Rangers on 30 October 2004 as substitute for an injured Danny Coyne and would take over the goalkeeping role for the following twenty-three Football League fixtures, with Burnley finishing in thirteenth place at the end of this campaign.

Disappointment also followed for Brian as he thought he had done enough to be selected for the Danish National squad that season.

At the commencement of the 2005–06 Football League season, Jensen made two appearances before being replaced by Danny Coyne for seven Football League appearances. Brian Jensen returned for the league home fixture against Ipswich Town, where he delivered a clean sheet in a 3–0 victory on 27 September 2005. He was to make a total of forty senior appearances that season, notably the 494 minutes he did not concede a league goal from 28 March to 22 April 2006, with Burnley finishing the season in seventeenth position.

With Jensen firmly instated for most of the 2006–07 football season, he made a total of thirty-two league and cup appearances for the season with Burnley once again finishing in the bottom half of the table in fifteenth position. Brian Jensen had in fact put in a transfer request in the January of that season, but due to negotiations and a return to first team duties he was taken off the list.

With the arrival of Hungarian goalkeeper Gabor Kiraly for the start of the 2007–08 Football League season Brian Jensen was left out of the side and did not return to first team duties until January 2008. Burnley Football Club in October 2007 appointed a new manager to replace Steve Cotterill with the appointment of Owen Coyle from Scottish League side St Johnstone. Brian Jensen completed the season under Owen Coyle with a total of twenty-one senior appearances, with Burnley finishing in thirteenth position.

The season of 2008–09 was to be memorable for Burnley Football Club and commenced with two league defeats, at Sheffield Wednesday followed by a home defeat to Ipswich Town. Progress was made in the Football League Cup with a visit to Chelsea in the fourth round tie in the November of 2008. Brian Jensen

Brian Jensen making one of his spectacular saves

who had played all of the League and Cup-ties in succession was to leave the field of play at Stamford Bridge that evening with his head held high. With the scores level after extra-time Brian Jensen was to make two penalty saves to secure Burnley's safe passage to the next round.

The season was full of expectation, with Burnley securely in the top half of the Football League Championship and a semi-final of the Football League Cup against Tottenham Hotspur, which was lost in the closing minutes of the second leg tie at Turf Moor. Brian Jensen was safely at the helm throughout this campaign,

missing only one League fixture. Burnley who finished the season in fifth position of the championship now qualified for the Play-offs with a two legged contest against Reading, which resulted in victory in both matches securing them a trip to Wembley, where Burnley overcame Sheffield United 1–0.

The Holy Grail, the Premier League awaited Burnley Football Club and Brian Jensen, who was consistent throughout this campaign, but the season ended in relegation after their first season back in the top Division.

With the return to the championship for the 2010–11 football season Burnley Football Club, now under manager Brian Laws, purchased goalkeeper Lee Grant from Sheffield Wednesday for £1million. He was to compete with Brian

Jensen throughout this season, with Brian making twenty-one championship appearances. In the January of 2011 another management change was made with the appointment of Eddie Howe who replaced Brian Laws. Burnley finished the season just out of the play offs in eighth position.

Brian Jensen, for the following 2011–12 season, was more or less back up to Lee Grant and made only four championship appearances throughout, with Burnley slipping into a thirteenth place finish.

In the October of the 2012–13 season, manager Eddie Howe resigned from his post and was replaced by ex Watford manager Sean Dyche. Brian Jensen was to make one last appearance for Burnley as sub to Lee Grant, in the final home fixture of the season against Ipswich Town. Sadly, his last farewell to a club he had served well in the ten years of his footballing career.

He moved on to play for Bury, Crawley Town and Mansfield Town.

DANNY COYNE
2004–07

Football League Appearances. 39

As Substitute 1

Football League Cup 4

Total Goals Conceded 45

Total Clean Sheets 13

Average Conceded per Game 1.05

Honours:

International Caps for Wales Whilst at Burnley 10

International Goals Conceded 8

Daniel Coyne was born on 27 August 1973 in Prestatyn, Wales. In his early youth career in 1992 he played for Tranmere Rovers, where he became first choice goalkeeper up until the end of 1999 making 111 Football League appearances

In the summer of 1999 he signed for First Division Grimsby Town where he would make one hundred and eighty-one Football League appearances in his four-year tenure. Whilst at Grimsby Town he was capped for Wales, the first of his sixteen caps in total. With Grimsby Town finishing at the bottom of the table at the end of the 2002–03 football season, Danny Coyne left the club for premier League side Leicester City.

At Leicester City he was understudy to first choice England International 'keeper, Ian Walker, and made a total of four Premier League Appearances before signing on a three-year deal for Burnley in July 2004. This was to be one of the first signings by new manager Steve Cotterill.

Danny Coyne was now first choice goalkeeper for the start of the 2004–05 Football League season and made his goalkeeping debut for Burnley in the Division One fixture at home to visitors Sheffield United on 7 August 2004.

Making their debuts that afternoon were defenders Michael Duff, John McGreal and Frank Sinclair with midfielder Micah Hyde. The result ended with a 1–1 drawn game.

Danny Coyne remained as first choice goalkeeper for the first eighteen senior games, which included two Football League Cup ties, recording a total of seven clean sheets. It was an injury at Queens Park Rangers in the championship fixture on 30 October that sidelined him for several months to be replaced by Brian Jensen. Danny Coyne returned from injury to represent Wales on 9 February 2005 in Cardiff against Hungary for the FIFA World Cup qualifiers, keeping a clean sheet in a 2–0 victory. This was to be the first of his ten caps whilst with Burnley for the following two seasons, which was to make him the most capped Burnley goalkeeper exceeding Colin McDonald's eight in the late 1950's.

His return to League Football was on 5 April 2005 for the home visit of West Ham United and was selected for a further three more championship fixtures to the end of this term.

At the start of the 2005–06 Championship season Danny Coyne was selected for seven of the first ten fixtures, but once again, at home to Brighton on 24 September, he suffered a knee injury and was substituted by Brian Jensen for the remainder of this game. He remained under treatment for the rest of this season, with Brian Jensen taking over the first team goalkeeping position.

The excellent form shown by goalkeeper Brian Jensen, restricted Danny Coyne's participation until the home fixture on 28 November 2006 against Leeds United, his first appearance for Burnley for fourteen months. He made a total of twelve goalkeeping appearances until the end of this 2006–07 campaign conceding just 13 goals. He was selected for Wales for four Internationals up until the end of

May 2007 conceding three goals with two clean sheets, positioning him as the clubs most capped goalkeeper.

It was confirmed at the end of that month that his contract would not be renewed and he was given a free transfer, which took him back to Tranmere Rovers for a second time. In his first season back with Rovers he recorded twenty clean sheets for the 2007–08 season in League One.

Up until the end of 2009 Danny Coyne made over eighty appearances for Tranmere Rovers before signing on a two-year deal at Middlesbrough where he made twenty-six appearances.

As well as a one-year stay at Sheffield United, unable to gain first team selection he moved to Shrewsbury Town in July 2013 and was appointed player coach. He also became joint assistant manager up until the end of 2014.

GÁBOR KIRÁLY
2007–2009

Gábor Ferenc Király was born in Szombathely, Hungary on 1 April 1976 and from 1998 to the present day has won selection for his national side Hungary over 100 times. He started his early junior career at his local side Haladás making a total of ninety-six appearances before stepping up and signing as second choice 'keeper for Hertha BSC of the German Bundesliga in 1997. He was eventually promoted to first team duties and throughout his seven year stay made over one hundred and ninety-eight goalkeeping appearances, and in the 1999–2000 Bundesliga season made ten UEFA Champions League appearances.

Premier League football club Crystal Palace made Gábor Király their first signing for the 2004–05 season and he made his debut for Palace in a Football League Cup tie at home to visitors Hartlepool United. He stayed at Palace who were relegated back to the championship at the end of that first season.

The following three seasons (that included being loaned out to West Ham United and Aston Villa) he made a total of one hundred League appearances up until the end of 2007.

After being released by Peter Taylor, Crystal Palace's manager, at the end of that season he joined Burnley on 30 May 2007 on a free transfer. He was immediately selected for the opening Football League Championship fixture at Turf Moor on 11 August 2007 against visitors West Bromwich Albion. In the Burnley selection

that day were defenders Jon Harley, Michael Duff, making his debut Stephen Jordan, with Wayne Thomas making his final appearance. In midfield were Steven Caldwell, Chris McCann, Wade Elliott and Joey Gudjonsson, with Robbie Blake and Andy Gray completing the forward line-up. The outcome was a 2–1 win for Burnley with Gábor Király firmly installed as first choice 'keeper in favour of Brian Jensen.

He had some outstanding performances at Burnley in his short stay at the club, and in the October of 2007 Steve Cotterill resigned as manager and was replaced weeks later by an unknown Owen Coyle from Scottish League side St Johnstone. He was prone to errors in some of the fixtures and with Brian Jensen restored to first team selection at the beginning of 2008 he too had a difficult time. Gábor Király was to play three final Championship matches, his final game for Burnley was on 15 March 2008.

Although he was retained for the 2008–09 football season, with the arrival of Peruvian goalkeeper Diego Penny he was now third choice 'keeper throughout this season and was loaned back to German Bundesliga side Bayer Leverkusen without making an appearance. He was transfer listed at the end of 2009 and was signed by German side TSV Munich 1860, where he made one hundred and sixty-eight league appearances.

He made a return to England in August 2014 and signed for championship side Fulham and made three appearances before finally returning to his homeland and his first club Haladás.

In the UEFA Euro Championship of 2016, Gábor Király became the oldest player ever at 40 years and 86 days to play in the competition. He helped his national side Hungary get into the last sixteen, but they were overcome by Belgium 4–0 after showing great promise.

He will always be remembered for wearing tracksuit bottoms at Burnley.

LEE GRANT
2005 AND 2010–13

Football League Appearances. . . . . .114 (+ 1 sub)

FA Cup Appearances 4

Football League Cup Appearances. 8

Total Goals Conceded 169

Total Clean Sheets 30

Average Conceded per Game 1.34

Lee Anderson Grant was born in Hemel Hempstead, Hertfordshire on 27 January 1983. He began his junior career at Watford Football Club in 1998, but could not make any impact with the club, and two years later in 2000 joined Derby County as a trainee goalkeeper. He made his debut for the Rams on 7 September 2002 in a home First Division fixture against Burnley, the club he would eventually join, which ended with Derby County losing 2–1. In his first season at Derby he made over thirty senior appearances and was also a regular in the England youth set up earning various caps, with his debut for England Under 21's on 9 September 2003 (the first of his four appearances).

Up until the end of the 2006–07 season Lee Grant had made a total of seventy-four appearances for Derby County with further loan appearances at Burnley and Oldham Athletic. He agreed to join Sheffield Wednesday in the July of 2007 where he signed a three-year contract for the championship side.

Throughout his three-year term at Wednesday he made a total of over one hundred and thirty-six senior appearances, and with his old boss Brian Laws now at Burnley, they made an offer of £1million for Lee Grant. He duly signed for Burnley on 27 July 2010.

At the commencement of the 2010–11 season, Brian Jensen was selected for first team goalkeeping duties, but with a Football League Cup tie at Morecambe

to be played on 24 August 2010 Lee Grant was selected for this tie, being his second debut for the club (his previous one was as a loanee) and ending in a 3–1 win for Burnley. In that side that evening were defenders Richard Eckersley, Clarke Carlisle, Leon Cort and Brian Easton. In midfield were David Edgar, Wade

Elliott, Jack Cork and Jay Rodriguez, with Steven Thompson and Chris Eagles completing the forward line-up.

It was not long through this first season before Lee Grant was elevated to first choice goalkeeper and made a total of thirty-one senior appearances to the end of his first season, which Burnley finishing in eighth place on their return to the Championship.

For the 2011–12 Football League Championship season, Lee Grant was installed throughout the campaign, that included a management change with Eddie Howe taking over from Brian Laws. Burnley were to finish in mid-table thirteenth position with Lee Grant making a total of forty-seven senior appearances (plus one as sub) of which five were cup tie appearances.

Within two months of the 2012–13 season Lee Grant was to play under his third manager with the arrival of Sean Dyche, former Watford coach who replaced AFC Bournemouth bound Eddie Howe. It was to be a turbulent time for Burnley Football Club, with half the bottom sides separated by four points with two games to go to the end of the season, meaning relegation was a possibility. Lee Grant was involved in all forty-six Football League Championship fixtures that season with Burnley finishing the campaign in eleventh position in the table, seven points clear of the relegated three.

His last appearance for Burnley was the final Championship home fixture to Ipswich Town and was fittingly subbed by Brian Jensen in the last appearances for both of these goalkeepers for Burnley.

Lee Grant became a firm favourite with the fans and was voted the clubs player of the year for 2012–13. He returned to his former football club Derby County for the start of the 2013–14 season on a three year contract and appeared for Derby County in all their Football League Championship and Cup ties throughout that season. In 2015/16 he lost his place to Scott Carson. He now plays for Stoke City having signed for them during the 2016-17 season (initially on loan) as understudy to Jack Butland. Butland's injury opened the door for Grant and he finally made his Premiership debut.

TOM HEATON
2013–17

Football League Appearances. 92

Premier League Appearances 73

FA Cup Appearances 6

Football League Cup Appearances. 3

Total Goals Conceded 188

Total Clean Sheets 60

Average Conceded per Game 1.08

Honours with Burnley:

Football League Championship Runners Up Medal . . . . .
2013–14

Football League Championship Winners Medal . 2015–16

International Caps for England 3

Total goals conceded. 4

Thomas David Heaton was born on 15 April 1986 in Chester, Cheshire. In his early youth he played both as a goalkeeper and as a midfielder. At the age of sixteen he signed junior terms at Manchester United and eventually made it to reserve standard making several appearances. Unable to gain a foothold in the United first team squad, he was on loan over a five season period with several Football League Clubs that included Swindon Town, Cardiff City, Queens Park Rangers, Rochdale and Wycombe Wanderers plus Manchester United feeder club, Royal Antwerp.

Over his eight-season career with United he gained several England caps at Under 16's and upwards, with a final total of nineteen caps. He owed a great deal to the coaching skills of his mentor Neil Bailey.

In the 2010–11 football season goalkeeper Tom Heaton signed for championship side Cardiff City on a two season contract and made a total of twenty-nine

league appearances. He was selected for Cardiff City in the Football League Cup Final at Wembley in the February of 2011 against Liverpool, and will always be remembered for the penalty shoot-out save from Steven Gerrard, with Cardiff City so close to winning this Final tie.

In the July of 2012 he signed for Bristol City and made forty-three appearances for them in that relegation season, his last being the away fixture at Burnley.

With Burnley Football Club manager Sean Dyche now in the hot seat for the commencement of the 2013–14 season, they purchased Tom Heaton from Bristol City and he made his goalkeeping debut in the opening home fixture against Bolton Wanderers on 3 August 2013. In the 1–1 drawn game were defenders Kieran Trippier, Danny Lafferty, Jason Shackell and Kevin Long. In midfield were Dean Marney, Ross Wallace and new signing David Jones. Making the forward line-up were Danny Ings, Sam Vokes and Junior Stanislas.

Burnley made a surprising start to the season, but for one incident at Brighton in late August when Tom Heaton was sent off and was replaced by Australian 'keeper Alex Cisak. Throughout the campaign he remained regular first choice 'keeper and was earning the recognition he deserved. In Tom Heaton's first twenty-five championship appearances he conceded 18 league goals, beating Jimmy Strong's first twenty-five Football League appearances of 19 in the 1946–47 season. He was now being compared to ex Burnley goalkeeping legend Alan Stevenson.

Burnley's season was going from strength to strength with the club at the top of the division, eventually finishing the season as runners-up to Leicester City and promotion back to the Premier League. Tom Heaton played a memorable part throughout, making a total of fifty senior appearances, conceding 43 goals and with a total of twenty clean sheets.

The 2014–15 Football Premier League season began for Tom Heaton and Burnley Football Club with the opening home fixture to visitors Chelsea, which ended with a 3–1 defeat. In the following four fixtures Tom Heaton was to keep three clean sheets with the only setback a 4–0 defeat at West Bromwich Albion; the highest total he would conceded that season. Burnley struggled throughout the campaign, and were unable to escape relegation. Tom Heaton made a total of forty senior appearances with a total of ten clean sheets in the Premier League season.

In England's pre-season tour of 2015 it was announced that Tom Heaton was to be selected for the squad (being the first Burnley player since Martin Dobson in 1974) with the prospect of being the first Burnley goalkeeper since Colin McDonald to win an England cap.

Burnley Football Club's returned to the Championship for season 2015–16, it was a slow start, going into the Christmas fixtures in eighth position. Following the 3–0 defeat at Hull City on Boxing Day, Burnley went twenty-three games without defeat and secured a top spot position and finally the championship title.

Goalkeeper Tom Heaton went from 2 to 27 February without conceding a league goal in 471 minutes of football, putting him in the all time record book for league matches in fifth place, equalling Alan Stevenson's 20 Football League clean sheets of the 1980–81 season and beating Jimmy Strong's nineteen in the 1946–47 season. Also, he became the first goalkeeper to captain the side on a permanent basis throughout that campaign.

He was once again selected for the England squad for the UEFA Euros of 2016 in France and made his England debut in the 87 minute at Sunderland against Australia, in a friendly on Friday 27 May. He is the fourth Burnley goalkeeper to be selected for England and follows in the footsteps of Jerry Dawson, Jack Hillman and Colin McDonald.

With Burnley's Football Clubs return to the Premier League for the commencement of the 2016/2017 season, Tom Heaton was for the second successive season honoured with the captains arm band.

Two new goalkeeping recruits were added to the squad ,Nick Pope from Charlton Athletic and Ex England goalkeeper Paul Robinson from Blackburn Rovers as back up to Tom Heaton who made some remarkable performances throughout that season particularly at Old Trafford on the 29 October against Manchester United.

He was subsequently named in England Manager Gareth Southgates squad for the international friendly at Wembley against Spain on 15 November and played the second half replacing team mate Joe Hart

Up until the four nil defeat at West Bromwich Tom Heaton had made a total of 142 League starts before being rested for two games with Paul Robinson taking over.

Throughout that season Burnley survived the threat of relegation and finally finished in sixteenth place six points clear of the bottom three with Tom Heaton and his defence keeping ten clean sheets equaling the ten that they recorded in their Premier League campaign two seasons previous.

Tom Heaton was voted Burnley Football Club player of the year for 2016/2017 and other supporters associations also voted him their player of the year.

In Englands final International of the season in Paris on the evening of 13th June 2017 Tom Heaton was selected for the first half of the International friendly against France, making it his third England selection and his first start.

Tom Heaton throughout the first half made three spectacular saves although two of these rebounded to gift France two of there first half goals giving them a 2-1 half time lead.

Stoke Citys Jack Butland took over the second half of this international with the outcome a 3-2 defeat for England.

Burnley's forthcoming 2017/2018 Premier League season will be Tom Heatons fifth season at the club.

OTHER GOALKEEPERS WHO HAVE PLAYED FOR BURNLEY

WILLIAM SMITH
1885–95

William S. Smith was born in Haggate, Lancashire and had a ten year spell at Burnley. He was the clubs first Football League goalkeeper playing in the very first game at Preston North End on 8 September 1888.

His final appearance was at Aston Villa on 6 April 1895. His later whereabouts are unknown.

His record for Burnley is:

Football League Appearances 7
Total Goals Conceded 26
Clean Sheets 0
Average Conceded per Game 3.71

ROBERT KAY
1884–88

Robert Kay (no known records of birth or whereabouts) was the second goalkeeper to be used in Burnley's inaugural season. His first game was at West Bromwich Albion on 29 September 1888 and his final appearance was at Notts County, where he conceded six goals, on 27 October 1888.

His record for Burnley is:

Football League Appearances 5
Total Goals Conceded 19
Total Clean Sheets 0
Average Conceded per Game 3.80

WILLIAM COX
1888–90

William Cox was brought to Burnley from Scottish football club Hibernian in November 1888 to steady the ship at Turf Moor, with the club already hemorrhaging a total of thirty-eight league goals in nine games and three 'keepers already used.

His first Football League game was a home fixture against West Bromwich Albion, on 10 November 1888 where he kept a clean sheet in a 2–0 victory. In his first full season he made thirteen Football League appearances and two FA Cup appearances.

He made another thirteen league appearances the following season, but conceded seven goals at Blackburn and nine at Wolverhampton Wanderers. His last game before joining Everton was at Derby County on 4 January 1890.

His record for Burnley is:

<pre>
Football League Appearances 26
FA Cup Appearances 2
Total Goals Conceded 80
Total Clean Sheets 4
Average Conceded per Game 2.86
</pre>

JAMES McCONNELL
1886–90

James McConnell came from Padiham and is the first 'keeper to be recorded in a Burnley team sheet for an FA Cup tie, when he made four appearances in this competition before the establishment of the Football League in 1888.

He made only one Football League appearance against Stoke on 11 January 1890 and his last appearance for Burnley was the FA Cup defeat at Sheffield United on 18 January 1890.

His record for Burnley is:

<pre>
Football League Appearances 1
FA Cup Appearances 5
</pre>

Total Goals Conceded 13

Total Clean Sheets 1

Average Conceded per Game 2.17

E. JOHNSON
1894–95

E. Johnson came from Glentoran in February 1894 as understudy to Jack Hillman. His first game for Burnley was at Turf Moor on 23 March 1894 in a 1–0 defeat to The Wednesday, which incidentally was England International Jack Yates last game for the club.

The following 1894–95 season he made eight Football League and one FA Cup appearances; his last at Stoke in a 5–1 away defeat on 30 March 1895. He returned to Glentoran at the end of this campaign, his whereabouts uncertain.

His record for Burnley is:

Football League Appearances 9

FA Cup Appearances 1

Total Goals Conceded 25

Total Clean Sheets 1

Average Conceded per Game 2.50

JAMES ARNOTT
1897–99

James Arnott's place and date of birth are unknown, but he came to Burnley from Hapton in 1897. He replaced David Haddow, who was transferred to New Brighton at the end of the 1897–98 season when promotion through the test matches was won. His first game was a 6–3 Football League home win on 7 March 1898 against Newton Heath.

The following league campaign he made eight First Division appearances and this was followed the following 1899–1900 season with three appearances, his last at Sheffield United on 11 November 1899.

His record for Burnley is:

Football League Appearances 12
Total Goals Conceded 23
Total Clean Sheets 3
Average Conceded per Game 1.92

ARCHIE PINNELL
1898–99

Archibald Pinnell, place and date of birth unknown, came to Burnley from Chorley in June 1898 for one season, returning to New Brompton the following July.

On Burnley's return to the First Division in the 1898–99 season, Archie Pinnell was selected for five of the fixtures, his first on the opening day at home to Notts County on 3 September 1898 in a 1–1 draw. His final game was at Newcastle United in a 4–1 defeat on 4 February 1899.

His record for Burnley is:

Football League Appearances 5
FA Cup Appearances 1
Total Goals Conceded 10
Total Clean Sheets 0
Average Conceded per Game 1.67

THOMAS SUGDEN
1901–02

Thomas Sugden's date and place of birth are unknown. His previous history and post Burnley whereabouts are also unknown.

He made his debut for Burnley against Leicester Fosse on 1 February 1902 in a Second Division fixture. He played a further six matches up until 15 March 1902, his last at Middlesbrough in a 3–0 defeat.

His record for Burnley is:

Football League Appearances 7

Total Goals Conceded 14

Total Clean Sheets 2

Average Conceded per Game 2.0

HARRY BROWN
1902

Harry Brown joined Burnley's first team squad from the juniors in March 1902. His debut was in a 1–0 home defeat to Bristol City on 22 March 1902.

He played the final seven games of the 1901–02 Second Division season, his last being in a 3–0 away defeat to Doncaster Rovers on 26 April 1902. He lasted a total of around six weeks in the job before finally being released, his whereabouts unknown.

His record for Burnley is:

Football League Appearances 7

Total Goals Conceded 11

Total Clean Sheets 1

Average Conceded per Game 1.57

FRED WYNNE
1902

Fred Wynne was born in Todmorden, his date of birth unknown, and joined Burnley in June 1902. His Second Division debut was on the opening game in the 1902–03 season away to Burton United on 1 September 1902.

He was to appear a further nine times until his final game at home to Woolwich Arsenal, which ended in a 3–0 defeat on 15 November 1902. His whereabouts after this game are unknown.

His record for Burnley is:

Football League Appearances 10

Total Goals Conceded 20

Total Clean Sheets 1

Total Average Conceded per Game 2.0

EDWIN TOWLER
1902–04

Edwin Towler, his place and date of birth unknown, joined Burnley in November 1902. His debut was a Second Division home game to Bristol City on 22 November 1902 where he kept a clean sheet in a 0–0 draw. He made 23 consecutive appearances to the end of that 1902–03 campaign which included an FA Cup tie at non-league Reading.

He was to appear one final time on 7 November 1903 in a 6–0 defeat at Bristol City. His whereabouts after this final game are unknown.

His record for Burnley is:

Football League Appearances 23
FA Cup Appearances............................. 1
Total Goals Conceded 59
Total Clean Sheets 2
Average Conceded per Game.................... 2.46

STEPHEN TILLOTSON
1909–11

Stephen Tillotson who was born in Brierfield, date unknown, was transferred to Burnley from Blackpool in August 1909 as a stand-in for Jerry Dawson. His debut was a Second Division fixture at home to Wolverhampton Wanderers, which ended in a 4–2 victory, and he was to make a further two appearances that 1909–10 season.

He made a further six appearances the following season, his last at Leicester Fosse on 8 April 1911 in a 1–1 drawn game. He was released at the end of that season.

His record for Burnley is:

Football League Appearances 9
Total Goals Conceded 9
Total Clean Sheets 4
Average Conceded per Game.................... 1.0

LEN MOORWOOD
1920–24

Len Moorwood was born in Wednesbury, Staffs in 1888 and was transferred to Burnley from West Bromwich Albion in October 1920 as back up for Jerry Dawson. He made his Football League debut on 7 May 1921 at Turf Moor for the visit of Sunderland. Burnley had already been made Football League Champions the previous week and he played this game in place of a rested Jerry Dawson.

The following campaign he made a total of five league appearances keeping two clean sheets. This was followed up in the 1922–23 season with a total of twelve league appearances, his final on 5 May 1923 for the visit of Birmingham City, which Burnley lost 2–0.

He was transferred in October 1924 to non league Weymouth being unable to regain any first team selection.

His record at Burnley was:

Football League Appearances 18

Total Goals Conceded 23

Total Clean Sheets 4

Average Conceded per Game 1.28

SAM PAGE
1923–25

Samuel Page was born in Blackheath, West Midlands in 1901 and was transferred to Burnley from Halesowen in November 1921 as cover for Jerry Dawson. When he made his Football League debut on 29 December 1923 against visitors Preston North End, nobody would have had an inkling that he would make a total of five senior appearances without conceding a goal (a record for a debut at the club).

From his debut to him first conceding a goal, to Birmingham in his sixth game, he played a total of 494 minutes, which included 30 minutes of extra-time in the FA Cup against Fulham, before any goal was recorded against him. He was to make a total of fourteen senior appearances for Burnley, his last at Sunderland on 2 May 1925.

He was transferred to Scottish league club St Johnstone at the end of that season. His record at Burnley was:

Football League Appearances. 12

FA Cup Appearances 2

Total Goals Conceded 15

Total Clean Sheets 6

Average Conceded per Game 1.07

THOMAS HAMPSON
1925–26

Thomas Hampson, born 20 May 1898, was transferred to Burnley from West Ham United in December 1925. He made his debut on 12 December 1925 in a Football League Division one home fixture against visitors Tottenham Hotspur, losing 2–1.

Four days later he was injured at Bury with the score 1–1. He was carried off, with Jack Hill and Len Hughes taking over, but Burnley still succumbed to an 8–1 thrashing. He played four more games to the end of this 1925–26 campaign, which included a high score against him at Sheffield United on 19 April 1926 in a 6–1 defeat.

His final game was at home against Cardiff City in the final match of the season, and he was subsequently released at the end of that term.

His record at Burnley was:

Football League Appearances 6

Total Goals Conceded 13

Total Clean Sheets 0

Average Conceded per Game 2.17

RICHARD TWIST
1931–32

Richard Twist, born in Hindsford, date of birth unknown, was signed by Burnley in November 1931, being another of Jerry Dawson's discoveries. He was signed up on amateur terms and was to play ten consecutive Second Division Football League games for Burnley.

His debut was the home visit of Millwall on 19 December 1931, which ended in a 1–1 draw. He played his last game at Manchester United on 17 February 1932, which Burnley lost 5–1, with George Sommerville returning for the following two league matches. The following October he signed for Preston North End.

His record at Burnley was:

```
Football League Appearances ....................  10
FA Cup Appearances...........................   1
Total Goals Conceded ..........................  31
Total Clean Sheets ...............................   0
Average Conceded per Game...................2.82
```

CHARLES HILLAM
1932–33

Charles Hillam was born locally in Burnley and joined from Clitheroe in May 1932 as stand-in for Herman Conway. His debut for Burnley was at Upton Park in a Second Division fixture on 19 October 1932 against West Ham United, which ended in a 4–4 draw. This game was of significance as Tom Jones scored all Burnley's four goals, making him the only player for the club to do so and not be on the winning side.

The most he conceded for Burnley was six at Chesterfield on 31 December 1932. Charles Hillam only stayed for one season before signing for Manchester United in May 1933.

His record at Burnley was:

```
Football League Appearances ....................  19
```

FA Cup Appearances 2

Total Goals Conceded 34

Total Clean Sheets 7

Average Conceded per Game 1.62

JOE MCNULTY
1949–52

Joseph McNulty, born 17 July 1923 in Dundalk, came to Burnley from Ards in May 1949. He made his First Division debut on 24 March 1951 as replacement for Jimmy Strong who was injured in the previous game against visitors Chelsea. His opponents on that March day were Manchester United, who won that fixture 2–1 at Turf Moor.

He kept a clean sheet the following week at Chelsea, but with Jimmy Strong's excellent recovery from injury, he lost his place until the conclusion of the following 1951–52 campaign when he made a further six Football League appearances. In his final game he conceded six away to Manchester United on 14 April 1952. He was subsequently transferred in June of that year to Sheffield United.

His record at Burnley was:

Football League Appearances 8

Total Goals Conceded 17

Total Clean Sheets 1

Average Conceded per Game 2.12

RODNEY JONES
1968–71

Rodney Jones, born 23 September 1945 in Ashton, was transferred to Burnley from Rotherham United in 1967. He made his debut at Fulham on 10 February 1968 in a 4–3 defeat, which was to be his only first team appearance of that campaign.

He made nine senior appearances the following 1968–69 season as Harry Thomson's understudy, but was unfortunately substituted in his final game at

Coventry City on 22 March 1969. He also conceded seven goals at Manchester City in his third appearance that season.

He was transferred to Rochdale in June 1971 after being unable to regain his first team place.

His record at Burnley was:

Football League Appearances 9
Football League Cup Appearances. 1
Total Goals Conceded 23
Total Clean Sheets 0
Average Conceded per Game 2.3

MIKE FINN
1974–76

Michael Finn, born 1 May 1954 in Liverpool, became an apprentice at Burnley in December 1971. He didn't make his debut until 13 March 1974 at Stamford Bridge against Chelsea in a 3–0 defeat. He made an appearance in the then third place Play off of the FA Cup at Leicester City, which was won by Burnley 1–0.

Mike was to play three more times the following 1974–75 season, his last against visitors Tottenham Hotspur on 12 April 1975, before finally being released by the club in May 1976.

His record at Burnley was:

Football League Appearances 4
FA Cup Appearances 1
Total Goals Conceded 10
Total Clean Sheets 1
Average Conceded per Game 2.0

WILLIAM O'ROURKE
1979–84

William J. O'Rourke, born 2 April 1960 in Nottingham, came to Burnley in February 1978 as an apprentice. He made his debut at Queens Park Rangers on 27 October 1979 in a 7–0 defeat. He only made one more appearance that season, as stand-in for Alan Stevenson,

In February 1982 he was on the wrong side of a 5–0 Football League Trophy semi-final beating by Wimbledon.

In the 1982–83 campaign he made a total of ten League Division Two appearances, which ended in relegation back to the Third Division after only one season. His last game for Burnley was at Crystal Palace on 17 May 1983 where a 1–0 defeat put paid to Burnley's chances of survival. He was transferred to Chester City in March 1984.

His record at Burnley was:

Football League Appearances	14
FA Cup Appearances	2
Football League Trophy Appearances	1
Total Goals Conceded	32
Total Clean Sheets	2
Average Conceded per Game	1.88

DENNIS PEACOCK
1985

Dennis Peacock was born 19 April 1953 in Lincoln, Lincolnshire. Dennis was brought to Burnley, on a loan spell from Doncaster Rovers, by manager Martin Buchan to cover for Joe Neenan. His debut for Burnley was at Peterborough on 28 September 1985, keeping a clean sheet in a 0–0 drawn game.

He made eight appearances for Burnley, which saw the introduction of another new manager, Tommy Cavanagh, replacing Martin Buchan. His final appearance was against visitors Southend United on 2 November in a Fourth Division fixture, which ended in a 3–1 defeat before completing his loan spell from Doncaster Rovers.

His record at Burnley was:

Football League Appearances 8

Total Goals Conceded 16

Total Clean Sheets 2

Average Conceded per Game 2.0

DAVID WILLIAMS
1988–94

David P. Williams was born on 18 September 1968 in Liverpool and was purchased by Burnley from Oldham Athletic in March 1988 as cover for Chris Pearce. He made his Football League debut at Grimsby Town on 8 April 1989, which ended in a 1–0 defeat, and made a further six league appearances that 1988–89 season.

Over the next few seasons he was called upon when Chris Pearce was unavailable, and was first choice keeper at the start of the 1992–93 season for the first two League and two Football League Cup games.

On 19 February 1991 he was on the wrong side of a 6–1 hammering from Preston North End in the northern semi-final of the Football League Trophy. His final appearance for Burnley was on 25 August 1992 in a Football League Cup fixture against visitors Carlisle United, which ended in a 1–1 drawn tie. He was transferred to Cardiff City in August 1994.

His record at Burnley was:

Football League Appearances 24

Football League Cup Appearances. 2

Football League Trophy Appearances 2

Total Goals Conceded 42

Total Clean Sheets 6

Average Conceded per Game 1.5

ANDREW MARRIOTT
1991

Andrew Marriott was born on 11 October 1970 in Sutton in Ashfield. He was loaned to Burnley in August 1991 from Nottingham Forest, as cover for Chris Pearce, for a three-month spell. His debut for Burnley was at Doncaster Rovers on 31 August 1991, which ended in a 4–1 victory.

A further fourteen Fourth Division League appearances and four Football League Trophy outings were made before being recalled for Forest in November 1991. His last Football League game was at Northampton Town on 30 November 1991.

His record at Burnley was:

Football League Appearances 15
Football League Trophy Appearances 2
Total Goals Conceded 17
Total Clean Sheets 7
Average Conceded per Game 1.12

NICKY WALKER
1992

Joseph Nicol Walker, born 29 September 1962 in Aberdeen, Scotland, was loaned to Burnley from Hearts in February 1992 as emergency cover for Chris Pearce. He made his debut for Burnley on 22 February against visitors Blackpool, which ended in a 1–1 draw.

He spent a four match period not conceding any goals, which included a Football League trophy fixture. His final appearance was at Mansfield Town before being recalled by Heart of Midlothian in March 1992.

His record for Burnley was:

Football League Appearances 6
Football League Trophy Appearances 1
Total Goals Conceded 4
Total Clean Sheets 5

Average Conceded per Game 0.57

WAYNE RUSSELL
1994–97

Wayne L. Russell was born on 29 November 1967 in Cardiff and joined Burnley from Ebbw Vale in October 1993. He was called upon as sub when Marlon Beresford was sent off in the Football League Division One match at Oldham on 27 August 1994.

In the 1994–95 relegation season under Jimmy Mullen, he made a total of six full Football League appearances plus another as sub when Beresford was sent off again at Portsmouth. He was also in the side that played a fifth round FA Cup home tie to Liverpool 28 January 1995, keeping a clean sheet in a 0–0 draw.

For the next few seasons he was understudy to Marlon Beresford and he made his final appearance for Burnley at Wycombe Wanderers in a 5–0 defeat on 15 April 1997. The club released him at the conclusion of that season.

His record for Burnley was:

Football League Appearances 22
As Substitute 2
FA Cup Appearances 1
Football League Cup Appearances 2
Total Goals Conceded 37
Total Clean Sheets 5
Average Conceded per Game 1.48

CHRIS WOODS
1998

Christopher C. E. Woods was born on 14 November 1959 in Boston, Lincolnshire. The ex England goalkeeper joined Burnley from Sunderland in July 1997 in a coaching capacity and back up for Marlon Beresford.

With the transfer of Marlon to Premier League Club Middlesbrough, Chris was invited to make his Burnley Division Two debut at Walsall on 7 March 1998, which ended in a clean sheet in a 0–0 drawn game. He completed the 1997–98 Division Two season making twelve consecutive Football League and two Football League Trophy appearances. Burnley narrowly escaped relegation that season, finishing twentieth in the division.

His record at Burnley was:

Football League Appearances 12

Football League Trophy Appearances 2

Total Goals Conceded 21

Total Clean Sheets 3

Average Conceded per Game 1.5

GAVIN WARD
1998

Gavin J. Ward, born on 30 June 1970 in Sutton Coldfield, was brought to Burnley on loan from Bolton Wanderers at the start of the 1998–99 season under new manager Stan Ternent. His debut for Burnley was at Chesterfield on 15 August 1998, which ended in a 1–0 defeat.

Stan Ternent was to make various changes during Gavin Wards stay at the club, which saw him sent back to Bolton in the November of this campaign with Paul Crichton taking over in goal.

His record at Burnley was:

Football League Appearances 17

Total Goals Conceded 24

Total Clean Sheets 2

Average Conceded per Game 1.41

MOST GOALS CONCEDED BY A BURNLEY GOALKEEPER

Jerry Dawson	10 versus	Aston Villa – 29 August 1925
George Sommerville	10 versus	Sheffield United – 19 January 1929
W. Cox	9 versus	Wolverhampton Wanderers – 7 December 1889
Jerry Dawson	8 versus	Manchester City – 24 October 1925
William Down	8 versus	Blackburn Rovers – 9 November 1929
George Sommerville	8 versus	Liverpool – 26 December 1928
George Sommerville	8 versus	Tottenham Hotspur – 1 September 1930
Harry Thomson	8 versus	West Bromwich Albion – 11 November 1967
Fred Poland	7 versus	Blackburn Rovers – 3 November 1888
W Cox	7 versus	Blackburn Rovers – 26 October 1889
Archie Kaye	7 versus	Everton – 27 December 1890
Archie Kaye	7 versus	Preston North End – 5 February 1891
David Haddow	7 versus	Stoke – 20 February 1896
George Sommerville	7 versus	Sunderland – 6 October 1926
George Sommerville*	7 versus	Bolton Wanderers – 5 November 1927
William Down	7 versus	Cardiff City – 1 September 1928
William Down	7 versus	Huddersfield Town 10 November 1928
George Sommerville	7 versus	Portsmouth – 4 January 1930
Alex Scott	7 versus	Bolton Wanderers – 2 January 1935
Tom Hetherington	7 versus	Leicester City – 13 March 1937
Ted Adams	7 versus	Arsenal – 20 February 1937

* Sommerville only actually conceded one of these goals as he was injured at 0-1 and had to leave the field. Two other players deputised.

Jimmy Strong	7	versus	Newcastle United – 15 September 1951
Colin McDonald	7	versus	Nottingham Forest – 18 September 1957
Adam Blacklaw	7	versus	Wolverhampton Wanderers – 13 April 1963
Harry Thomson	7	versus	Sheffield Wednesday – 6 May 1967
Harry Thomson	7	versus	Tottenham Hotspur – 7 September 1968
Rodney Jones	7	versus	Manchester City – 7 December 1968
Billy O'Rourke	7	versus	Queens Park Rangers – 27 October 1979
Marlon Beresford	7	versus	Watford – 5 April 2003

BURNLEY'S FULL INTERNATIONAL GOALKEEPERS

Danny Coyne	Wales	10
Colin McDonald	England	8
Adam Blacklaw	Scotland	3
Tom Heaton	England	3
Jerry Dawson	England	2
Nikalaos Michopoulos	Greece	2
Jack Hillman	England	1

MOST MINUTES NOT CONCEDING (LEAGUE ONLY)

Jimmy Strong	16 November 1946 – 26 December 1946	675 mins
Alan Stevenson	30 August 1980 – 7 October 1980	675 mins
Alan Stevenson	31 March 1973 – 28 April 1973	510 mins
Brian Jenson	28 March 2006 – 22 April 2006	494 mins
Tom Heaton	2 February 2016 – 27 February 2016	471 mins
William Green	11 February 1905 – 1 April 1905	445 mins
Jerry Dawson	27 November 1920 – 27 December 1920	441 mins
Alan Stevenson	11 November 1972 – 23 December 1972	436 mins
Marlon Beresford	25 February 1997 – 22 March 1997	434 mins
Jimmy Strong	18 January 1947 – 15 March 1947	434 mins

MOST MINUTES NOT CONCEDING (ALL COMPETITIONS)

Jimmy Strong	18 January 1947 – 1 March 1947	680 mins
Jimmy Strong	16 November 1946 – 26 December 1946	675 mins
Alan Stevenson	2 September 1980 – 7 October 1980	660 mins
Alan Stevenson	31 March 1973 – 28 April 1973	510 mins
Brian Jensen	28 March 2006 – 22 April 2006	494 mins
Sam Page	29 December 1923 – 9 February 1924	494 mins
Tom Heaton	2 February 2016 – 27 February 2016	471 mins
Harry Thomson	19 October 1968 – 16 November 1968	470 mins
Jerry Dawson	11 February 1922 – 11 March 1922	454 mins
William Green	11 February 1905 – 1 April 1905	445 mins

OTHER BURNLEY GOALKEEPING FACTS

In the very first Football League season of 1888–89, Burnley selected centre-forward Fred Poland as goalkeeper for the visit of Blackburn Rovers on 3 November 1889, which ended in a 7–1 defeat.

Forward player Billy Bowes was selected in goal for the first half of the away fixture at West Bromwich Albion on 7 January 1893, due to the absence of first choice 'keeper Jack Hillman. When Jack Hillman finally took up his position for the second half, Burnley were already four goals down, with the final result ending in a 7–1 defeat.

All rounder Walter Place senior, Burnley's outside-left, was selected for two Football League fixtures as goalkeeper; his first for the away fixture at Blackburn Rovers on 18 November 1893 followed seven days later at Everton, both ending in defeat with seven goals conceded in total.

When goalkeeper William Tatham was injured in the Football League away fixture at Preston North End on 26 September 1896, he was replaced by outside-left Walter Place senior who saved two penalties as well as keeping a clean sheet in this 5–3 defeat for Burnley.

With Burnley facing relegation at the end of the 1899–1900 Football League season, goalkeeper Jack Hillman was accused of offering a bribe to the Nottingham Forest players to take things easy in Burnley's away fixture on 28 April 1900. He was subsequently found guilty of the offence and banned from football for an entire season.

New goalkeeper signing William Green from Brentford for the commencement of the 1903–04 Football League Division Two season makes his first four goalkeeping appearances for Burnley without conceding a goal and it wasn't until the fifth fixture at Preston North End on 26 September 1903 that he first conceded in the thirteenth minute.

In the 1923–24 football season goalkeeper Sam Page made his goalkeeping debut for Burnley. In his first three league fixtures plus two FA Cup fixtures he went a total of 480 minutes without conceding a goal. He finally conceded in his sixth appearance for the club in the First Division fixture against Birmingham on 9 February 1924 in the fourteenth minute to make it a total of 494 minutes without conceding.

Jerry Dawson plays his final game for Burnley on Christmas Day 1928 at the age of 40 with Burnley beating visitors Liverpool 3–2 in a League Division One fixture.

In tragic circumstances in a First Division fixture at Ewood Park on 9 November 1929, Burnley 'keeper William Down was severely injured in a clash with a Blackburn Rovers forward. Although he carried on throughout this 8–3 defeat for Burnley, he subsequently collapsed after the fixture and was hospitalised, lucky to have survived. He never recovered his form and was released by the club at the end of that season in 1930.

Ted Adams made his goalkeeping debut for Burnley after coming out of retirement at the age of 29 for the Second Division fixture on 29 February 1936 at Turf Moor against visitors West Ham United. He went on to make a further 117 appearances before the outbreak of World War II.

Another of Burnley's finest goalkeepers Colin McDonald, never fully recovered his fitness after recovering from an injury he sustained whilst representing the Football League against The League of Ireland in Dublin on 17 March 1959. He never played for Burnley again, although he had brief spells at Bury and Altrincham.

In an impressive debut for Burnley on 9 August 1969, goalkeeper Peter Mellor was injured in the final minutes of this 0–0 drawn fixture at Derby County. He was replaced by full-back Les Latcham for the remainder of this First Division fixture.

In a Football League Division Three fixture on 27 December 1980 against Blackpool at Turf Moor, Burnley goalkeeper Alan Stevenson becomes the first 'keeper to be sent off for the club after fouling an opponent.

Wayne Russell becomes Burnley's first goalkeeper to make his debut as a substitute, replacing Marlon Beresford who was dismissed for handling the ball outside his area at Oldham on 27 August 1994 in a Third Division League fixture.

Goalkeeper Tom Heaton becomes the first 'keeper to captain the club for the entire 2015–16 season with Burnley winning the Championship and returning to the Premier League. He also equalled Alan Stevenson's twenty clean sheets of the 1980–81 season in league games only.

Ex Burnley goalkeeper Gábor Király, who left the club in 2009, made several appearance for Hungary in the UEFA Euros in France 2016. He became the oldest player of all time at the age of 40 years and 86 days to play in this competition.

BURNLEY GOALKEEPERS BY NUMBERS

0   No Burnley 'keeper has ever scored a goal in the clubs entire history, although Jerry Dawson came close in an FA Cup tie at Barnsley on 4 February 1911 when he took a penalty-kick for Burnley and missed.

1   On his goalkeeping debut for Burnley at Wolverhampton Wanderers on 2 September 1895, goalkeeper Walter Napier was so badly injured that he never played for the club again after his one and only game.

2   Only two outfield players have ever been chosen to represent Burnley in goal for a full ninety minutes of football, the first being forward Fred Poland, who conceded seven goals in the Football League fixture with the visit of Blackburn Rovers on 3 November 1888. Winger and all rounder, Walter Place senior, became the second when he was selected for the Football League fixture at Blackburn Rovers on 18 November 1893 which Burnley lost 3–2. He was also selected seven days later for the Football League fixture at Everton, which Burnley lost 4–3.

3   A total of three goalkeepers throughout their Burnley career have had over 100 clean sheets.

4   Tom Heaton became the fourth Burnley goalkeeper to represent England when he was called upon as sub for the International friendly against Australia at Sunderland in the 87th minute on 27 May 2016. He follows in the footsteps of past Burnley goalkeepers to have represented England, Jack Hillman, Jerry Dawson and Colin McDonald.

6   A nightmare goalkeeping debut for Burnley goalkeeper Anthony Woodworth on his debut and one and only appearance for the club against Hereford United on 24 January 1987 at Turf Moor, which ended with a 6–0 defeat..

7   Burnley have had a total of seven goalkeepers who have represented their national side on international duties. Four of these have represented England – Jack Hillman, Jerry Dawson, Colin McDonald and Tom Heaton, Adam Blacklaw has represented Scotland, Nik Michopoulos for Greece and Danny Coyne for Wales.

9   Only one goalkeeper has conceded nine goals for Burnley. In a Football League fixture at Wolverhampton Wanderers, W. Cox conceded nine in Burnley's 9–1 defeat on 7 December 1889.

10   A total of 10 goals have been conceded twice in Burnley's entire 134 season history. The first was at Aston Villa on 29 August 1925 when Jerry Dawson conceded 10 in a First Division fixture. This was followed on 19 January 1929 when George Sommerville conceded 10 goals at Sheffield United in a First Division fixture.

11   In Burnley Club's first ever FA Cup Tie at Darwen Old Wanderers, on 7 October 1885, because of restrictions on professional players representing their clubs, an all-amateur side represented Burnley in this 11–0 defeat of which no records of players picked were recorded.

13   Throughout Burnley Football Club's entire history, thirteen goalkeepers have made just one senior appearance.

14   Only fourteen outfield players have been used as substitutes for goalkeepers in all of Burnley Football Club's senior appearances. The first being Billy Bowes, who made his appearance in the first half of the First Division fixture at West Bromwich Albion on 7 January 1893, in which he conceded four goals.

17   Seventeen goalkeepers have made over a hundred senior appearances in all Burnley's senior fixtures.

20   Burnley goalkeeper, George Sommerville, conceded 20 goals in four Football League Division One fixtures from 26 December 1928 until 19 January 1929. Although he kept a clean sheet in the third of these four fixtures.

25   Burnley goalkeeper Jimmy Strong recorded twenty-five clean sheets throughout the 1946–47 football season with six of these coming from FA Cup ties.

40   Jerry Dawson, Burnley Football Club's oldest goalkeeper to have played for the club made his final appearance on 25 December 1928 in a First Division fixture against visitors Liverpool, which ended with a 3–2 victory for Burnley.

45   Jerry Dawson made 45 FA Cup appearances

60   Goalkeeper, Adam Blacklaw, made a total of sixty senior appearances in the 1960–61 football season. A club record!

90   A total of ninety recorded goalkeepers have represented Burnley in all the club's senior fixtures (this does not include substitutes or the unrecorded 'keeper for the club's first away FA Cup tie at Darwen in October 1885).

98   A total of 98 goals were conceded by Burnley keeper Adam Blacklaw out of a total of 60 senior appearances in the 1960–61 football season.

203   Burnley goalkeeper, Jimmy Strong, made a total of 203 consecutive Football League appearances from 31 August 1946 until 23 March 1951.

500   Burnley's 500th clean sheet was recorded by goalkeeper Jimmy Strong, in the Second Division fixture at Upton Park against West Ham United on the 31 May 1947.

543   Total senior goalkeeping appearances were made by Alan Stevenson from 23 January 1972 to 30 April 1983.

568   Total senior goalkeeping appearances by Jerry Dawson from 13 April 1907 to 25 December 1928.

1,000   Burnley's 1,000th clean sheet was recorded by goalkeeper Phillip Harrington on 9 November 1985 at Cambridge United in a Fourth Division fixture which Burnley won 4–0.

1,458   Total clean sheets recorded by all of Burnley's goalkeepers from 15 October 1887 until 29th April 2017.

5,000   Burnley's 5,000th conceded goal was recorded on 4 September 1976 in a Division Two fixture at Hereford United when goalkeeper Gerry Peyton conceded in the 90 minute.

7,922   Total goals conceded by all of Burnley's goalkeepers from 7 October 1885 to 19 April 2016.

1,000,000   The first £1,000,000 purchase by Burnley for a goalkeeper was to Sheffield Wednesday for 'keeper Lee Grant in July 2010.

BURNLEY'S GOALKEEPERS
FROM 1886 TO 2017

Nationality	Name	League	FA Cup	FL Cup	Other	Total	Total Clean Sheets	Total Goals Conceded
English	Adams, Edward	111	7			118	36	164
English	Arnott, James	12				12	3	23
English	Ashbridge, Kenneth	1				1	0	4
English	Ashcroft, Gordon	1				1	0	1
English	Beresford, Marlon	286	25	22	16	349	77	500
English	Birchenough, Frank	2				2	0	3
Scottish	Blacklaw, Adam	318	44	12	9	383	93	570
English	Breedon, Jack		1			1		1
English	Brown, Harry	7				7	1	11
German	Cennamo, Luigi		1(sub)			1(sub)		2
English	Crichton, Paul	82 (1)	4	4	2	92 (1)	30	120
Australian	Cisak, Ale	0 (1)		1		1 (1)	1	1

Nationality	Name	League	FA Cup	FL Cup	Other	Total	Total Clean Sheets	Total Goals Conceded
English	Collins, Henry	30	3			33	15	28
English	Conway, Herman	81	6			87	17	148
Scottish	Cox, W	26	2			28	4	80
Welsh	Coyne, Daniel	39 (1)		4		43 (1)	12	45
English	Dawson. Jerry	522	45		1	568	164	794
English	Down, William	80	2			82	11	185
English	Drabell, Frank	2				2		4
English	Finn, Michael	4	1			5	1	10
	Foxcroft, George		1			1		3
English	Furnell, Jim	2		1		3		6
English	Gilks, Mathew			2		2	0	2
English	Grant, Lee	114 (1)	4	8		126 (1)	30	169
English	Green, William	147	6			153	44	222
Scottish	Haddow, David	38	5		4	47	15	55
English	Hampson, Thomas	6				6		13
English	Hansbury, Roger	83	8	6	6	103	22	154
Welsh	Harrington, Philip	2				2	1	1
English	Heaton, Tom	165	6	3		174	60	188

163

Nationality	Name	League	FA Cup	FL Cup	Other	Total	Total Clean Sheets	Total Goals Conceded
English	Hetherington, Thomas	67				67	16	105
English	Hillam, Charles	19	2			21	7	34
English	Hillman, Jack	175	9		4	188	57	256
Danish	Jensen, Brian	267 (4)	17	19	3	306 (4)	88	416
Irish	Johnson., E	9	1			10	1	25
English	Jones, Rodney	9		1		10		23
	Kay, Robert	5				5		19
Scottish	Kaye, Archibald	28	2			30	4	74
Welsh	Kendall, Mark	2	1			3	1	7
Hungarian	Király, Gábor	27	1	1		29	6	38
Norwegian	Kval, Frank		1			1		3
English	Lovett, Jonathon	1				1		3
English	Marriott, Andrew	15			4	19	7	17
English	McConnell, James	1	5			6	1	13
English	McDonald, Colin	186	15			201	52	272
Irish	McNulty, Joseph	8				8	1	17

Nationality	Name	League	FA Cup	FL Cup	Other	Total	Total Clean Sheets	Total Goals Conceded
English	Mellor, Peter	69	4	8		81	19	107
Greek	Michopoulos, Nikalaos	85	5	3		93	32	122
English	Moorwood, Len	18				18	4	24
Scottish	Napier, Walter	1				1		5
English	Neenan, Joe	90	3	4	7	104	21	156
English	O'Rourke, William	14	2		1	17	2	32
English	Page, Sam	12	2			14	6	15
Welsh	Parton, Jeffrey	3				3		7
English	Parks, Anthony			2		2		5
English	Peacock, Denis	8				8	2	16
Welsh	Pearce, Christopher	181	15	16	20	232	74	280
English	Peyton, Gerry	30	1	1	2	34	10	48
Peruvian	Penny, Diego	1 (1)		1 (1)		2 (2)		7
English	Pinnell, Archibald	5	1			6		10
English	Place (Senior), Walter	2				2		7
Scottish	Poland, Fred	1				1		7
English	Pollitt, Michael	4				4	1	5

Nationality	Name	League	FA Cup	FL Cup	Other	Total	Total Clean Sheets	Total Goals Conceded
	Porterfield, Alfred	2				2		5
Welsh	Russell, Wayne	22(2)	1	2		25 (2)	5	37
	Ryan, William	1				1		1
English	Scott, Alex	57	8			65	17	104
English	Sewell, George	23	4			27	10	37
English	Smith, William	7				7		26
English	Sommerville, George	118	6			124	18	265
English	Stevenson, Alan	438	33	36	33	540	151	717
English	Strong, Jimmy	264	21			285	103	294
	Sugden, Thomas	7				7	2	14
English	Tatham, William	51	2			53	14	88
English	Thompson, Desmond	62	7			69	15	99
Scottish	Thomson, Harry	117	5	15	4	141	38	221
English	Tillotson, Stephen	9				9	4	9
	Towler, Edwin	23	1			24	2	59
English	Twist, Richard	10	1			11		31

Nationality	Name	League	FA Cup	FL Cup	Other	Total	Total Clean Sheets	Total Goals Conceded
English	Waiters, Tony	38	1	1	2	42	9	66
Scottish	Walker, Nicol	6			1	7	5	4
English	Ward, Gavin	17				17	2	24
	Welsh, Fred	1				1		3
	Whittaker, Edgar	1				1		2
English	Williams, David	24		2	2	28	6	42
English	Woods, Christopher	12			2	14	3	20
English	Woodworth, Anthony	1				1		6
English	Wynne, Fred	10				10	1	20

OUTFIELD PLAYERS WHO HAVE SUBSTITUTED FOR GOALKEEPERS

Nationality	Name	League	FA Cup	FL Cup	Other	Total Clean Sheets	Total Goals Conceded
English	Bowes, Billy	1					4
English	Farrell, Andy	1				1	0
English	Freeman, Paddy	1					4
English	Hill, Jack	2					4
English	Hughes, Len	1					5
English	Latcham, Les	2				1	1
English	Laws, Brian	2				1	2
Irish	McGee, Paul	1					1
English	Mather, Harry	1				1	0
English	Monington, Mark	1				1	0
English	Place (senior), Walter	1					0
English	Spicer, John	1					2
Scottish	Taylor, David	1					3
Scottish	Winton, Doug	1					1

BURNLEY FOOTBALL CLUB SEASON ON SEASON GOALKEEPING STATISTICS 1886–2016

Season	Goalkeeper	League	FA Cup Apps	FL Cup Apps	Other	Total Clean Sheets	Total Goals Conceded
1886–87	James McConnell		2				5
1887–88	James McConnell		2			1	3
1888–89 Football League 9th 17pts	William Smith Robert Kay Fred Poland W. Cox	3 5 1 13	2			4	12 19 7 32
1889–90 Football League 11th 13pts	W. Cox William Smith James McConnell Archibald Kaye	13 2 1 6	1			3	48 7 5 7

Season	Goalkeeper	League	FA Cup Apps	FL Cup Apps	Other	Total Clean Sheets	Total Goals Conceded
1890–91 Football League 8th 21pts	Archibald Kaye	22	2			1	67
1891–92 Football League 7th 26pts	Jack Hillman	26	2			7	49
1892–93 First Division 6th 30pts	Jack Hillman William Smith William Ryan Billy Bowes (sub)	28 1 1 1	2			10	38 2 1 4
1893–94 First Division 5th 34pts	Jack Hillman Walter Place Sr. E. Johnson	27 2 1	1			6	44 7 1
1894–95 First Division 9th 26pts	Jack Hillman E. Johnson William Smith Alfred Porterfield	19 8 1 2	1			6 1	24 24 5 5
1895–96 First Division 10th 27pts	Walter Napier William Tatham David Haddow	1 25 4	1 2			10	5 33 15

Season	Goalkeeper	League	FA Cup Apps	FL Cup Apps	Other	Total Clean Sheets	Total Goals Conceded
1896–97 First Division 16th 19pts (rel)	William Tatham	20	1			2	44
	David Haddow	10			4	2	22
	Walter Place Sen (sub)	1					0
1897–98 Second Division 1st 48pts (prom) champions	David Haddow	24	3			13	18
	James Arnott	1			4		3
	Jack Hillman	5				3	10
1898–99 First Division 3rd 39pts	Archie Pinnell	5	1				10
	William Tatham	2					8
	James Arnott	8				2	10
	Jack Hillman	19	1			8	23
1899–1900 First Division 17th 27pts (rel)	Jack Hillman	31	1			7	45
	James Arnott	3				1	10
1900–01 Second Division 3rd 44pts	Henry Collins	30	3			15	28
	William Tatham	4				2	3

171

Season	Goalkeeper	League	FA Cup Apps	FL Cup Apps	Other	Total Clean Sheets	Total Goals Conceded
1901–02 Second Division 9th 30pts	Jack Hillman Thomas Sugden Harry Brown	20 7 7	2			10 2 1	23 14 11
1902–03 Second Division 18th 20pts	Fred Wynne Fred Welsh Edgar Whittaker Edwin Towler	10 1 1 22	1			1 2	20 3 2 53
1903–04 Second Division 5th 39pts	William Green Edwin Towler	33 1	2			12	52 6
1904–05 Second Division 11th 30pts	William Green	34	2			9	56
1905–06 Second Division 9th 38pts	William Green Jonathon Lovett	37 1	1			10	52 3
1906–07 Second Division 7th 40pts	William Green Jerry Dawson	37 1	1			12 1	50 0
1907–08 Second Division 7th 46pts	William Green Jerry Dawson	4 34	1			10	9 43

Season	Goalkeeper	League	FA Cup Apps	FL Cup Apps	Other	Total Clean Sheets	Total Goals Conceded
1908–09 Second Division 14th 33pts	Jerry Dawson William Green	36 2	6			11 1	60 3
1909–10 Second Division 14th 34pts	Jerry Dawson Stephen Tillotson	35 3	2			8 1	59 4
1910–1911 Second Division 8th 41pts	Jerry Dawson Stephen Tillotson	32 6	4			10 3	41 5
1911–12 Second Division 3rd 52pts	Jerry Dawson	38	1			13	43
1912–13 Second Division 2nd 50pts (prom)	Jerry Dawson Ron Sewell Frank Drabell	30 6 2	6			10 1 1	47 9 4
1913–14 First Division 12th 36pts	Jerry Dawson Ron Sewell David Taylor (sub)	32 6 1	6 2			14 3	43 11 3
1914–15 First Division 4th 43pts	Jerry Dawson Ron Sewell	35 3	3			14 1	46 4

173

Season	Goalkeeper	League	FA Cup Apps	FL Cup Apps	Other	Total Clean Sheets	Total Goals Conceded
1919–20 First Division 2nd 51pts	Jerry Dawson	34	2			10	49
	Ron Sewell	8	2			5	13
1920–21 First Division 1st 59pts Champions	Jerry Dawson	39	3			15	41
	Frank Birchenough	2			1		3
	Len Moorwood	1					2
1921–22 First Division 3rd 49pts	Jerry Dawson	37	2			13	54
	Len Moorwood	5				2	5
1922–23 First Division 15th 38pts	Jerry Dawson	30	1			9	45
	Len Moorwood	12				2	17
1923–24 First Division 17th 36pts	Jerry Dawson	36	5			10	61
	Sam Page	6	2			5	6
1924–25 First Division 19th 34pts	Jerry Dawson	36	1			11	68
	Sam Page	6				1	9

Season	Goalkeeper	League	FA Cup Apps	FL Cup Apps	Other	Total Clean Sheets	Total Goals Conceded
1925–26 First Division 20th 36pts	Jerry Dawson	35	2			5	91
	Thomas Hampson	6					13
	Gordon Ashcroft	1					1
	Jack Hill (sub)	1					2
	Len Hughes (sub)	1					5
1926–27 First Division 5th 47pts	George Sommerville	41	3			11	82
	Jerry Dawson	1					1
1927–28 First Division 19th 39pts	George Sommerville	13				1	28
	William Down	29	1			3	66
	Jack Hill (sub)	1					2
	Paddy Freeman (sub)	1					4
1928–29 First Division 19th 38pts	George Sommerville	4	2			1	24
	Jerry Dawson	1					2
	William Down	37	1			5	84
1929–30 First Division 21st 36pts (rel)	George Sommerville	28	1			1	63
	William Down	14				3	35
1930–31 Second Division 8th 45pts	George Sommerville	13				6	29
	Herman Conway	29	2				50

Season	Goalkeeper	League	FA Cup Apps	FL Cup Apps	Other	Total Clean Sheets	Total Goals Conceded
1931–32 Second Division 19th 35pts	Herman Conway Richard Twist George Sommerville	13 10 19	1			2 4	21 31 39
1932–1933 Second Division 19th 36pts	Herman Conway Charles Hillam	23 19	2 2			4 7	48 34
1933–1934 Second Division 13th 42pts	Herman Conway Thomas Hetherington Alex Scott	16 15 11	2			5 4 1	29 25 21
1984–35 Second Division 12th 41pts	Alex Scott Thomas Hetherington	28 14	6			10 1	56 25
1935–36 Second Division 15th 37 pts	Thomas Hetherington Alex Scott Ted Adams Kenneth Ashbridge	11 18 12 1	2			2 6 3	17 27 13 4
1936–37 Second Division 13th 42pts	Thomas Hetherington Ted Adams	26 16	3			9 6	37 34
1937–38 Second Division 6th 44pts	Thomas Hetherington Ted Adams	1 41	3			16	1 58

Season	Goalkeeper	League	FA Cup Apps	FL Cup Apps	Other	Total Clean Sheets	Total Goals Conceded
1938–39 Second Division 14th 39pts	Ted Adams	42	1			11	59
1945–1946 Second Division	George Foxcroft Jack Breedon		1 1				3 1
1946–47 Second Division 2nd 58pts (prom)	Jimmy Strong	42	9			25	32
1947–48 First Division 3rd 52pts	Jimmy Strong	42	1			17	45
1948–49 First Division 15th 38pts	Jimmy Strong	42	3			16	55
1949–50 First Division 10 45pts	Jimmy Strong	42	3			17	44
1950–51 First Division 10th 42pts	Jimmy Strong Joseph McNulty	40 2	1			12 1	43 2

177

Season	Goalkeeper	League	FA Cup Apps	FL Cup Apps	Other	Total Clean Sheets	Total Goals Conceded
1951–52 First Division 14th 40pts	Jimmy Strong	36	4			12	51
	Joseph McNulty	6					15
1952–53 First Division 6th 48pts	Jimmy Strong	20	4			4	24
	Des Thompson	22				8	32
	Harry Mather (sub)	1					0
1953–54 First Division 7th 46pts	Des Thompson	37	3			6	63
	Colin McDonald	5				1	9
1954–55 First Division 10th 43pts	Colin McDonald	39	1			15	45
	Des Thompson	3				1	4
1955–56 First Division 7th 44pts	Colin McDonald	42	6			14	60
1956–57 First Division 7th 46pts	Colin McDonald	34	5			9	39
	Adam Blacklaw	8				4	14
	Doug Winton (sub)	1					1
1957–58 First Division 6th 47pts	Colin McDonald	39	3			8	70
	Adam Blacklaw	3					11

Season	Goalkeeper	League	FA Cup Apps	FL Cup Apps	Other	Total Clean Sheets	Total Goals Conceded
1958–59 First Division 7th 48pts	Colin McDonald Adam Blacklaw	27 15	5			5 3	49 25
1959–60 First Division 1st 55pts (champions)	Adam Blacklaw Jim Furnell	41 1	8			13	69 1
1960–61 First Division 4th 51pts	Adam Blacklaw Jim Furnell	41 1	7	7 1	5	16	98 5
1961–1962 First Division 2nd 53pts	Adam Blacklaw	42	8			10	75
1962–63 First Division 3rd 54pts	Adam Blacklaw	42	3			12	60
1963–64 First Division 9th 44pts	Adam Blacklaw	42	5			11	71
1964–65 First Division 12th 42pts	Adam Blacklaw Harry Thomson	34 8	5			7 3	66 8

Season	Goalkeeper	League	FA Cup Apps	FL Cup Apps	Other	Total Clean Sheets	Total Goals Conceded
1965–66 First Division 3rd 55pts	Harry Thomson	15		2		5	22
	Adam Blacklaw	27	3	3		10	37
1966–67 First Division 14th 39pts	Adam Blacklaw	23		2	4	7	44
	Harry Thomson	19	2	1	4	9	42
1967–68 First Division 14th 38pts	Harry Thomson	41	1	5		11	77
	Rodney Jones	1					4
1968–69 First Division 14th 39pts	Harry Thomson	34	2	7	2	10	72
	Rodney Jones	8		1			19
	Les Latcham (sub)	1					1
1969–70 First Division 14th 39pts	Peter Mellor	42	3	5		12	68
	Les Latcham (sub)	1					0
1970–71 First Division 21st 27pts (rel)	Tony Waiters	35	1	1	2	9	61
	Peter Mellor	7				1	12
1971–72 Second Division 7th 46pts	Tony Waiters	3		3			5
	Peter Mellor	20	1			6	27
	Alan Stevenson	17				5	22
	Jeff Pardon	2					4

Season	Goalkeeper	League	FA Cup Apps	FL Cup Apps	Other	Total Clean Sheets	Total Goals Conceded
1972–73 Second Division 1st 62pts (prom) champions	Alan Stevenson	42	2	1	2	20	44
1973–74 First Division 6th 46pts	Alan Stevenson	40	5	3	8	19	62
	Jeff Pardon	1					3
	Michael Finn	1	1			1	3
1974–75 First Division 10th 45pts	Alan Stevenson	39	1	3		10	66
	Michael Finn	3					7
1975–76 First Division 21st 28pts (rel)	Alan Stevenson	22	1	5		6	43
	Gerry Peyton	20				6	28
1976–77 Second Division 16th 36pts	Gerry Peyton	10		1	2	4	20
	Alan Stevenson	32	3		1	12	52
1977–78 Second Division 11th 40pts	Alan Stevenson	42	2	4	3	10	80

Season	Goalkeeper	League	FA Cup Apps	FL Cup Apps	Other	Total Clean Sheets	Total Goals Conceded
1978–79 Second Division 13th 40pts	Alan Stevenson	42	4	3	9	12	81
1979–80 Second Division 21st 27pts (rel)	Alan Stevenson William O'Rourke	40 2	2	2	3	8	75 9
1980–81 Third Division 8th 50pts	Alan Stevenson William O'Rourke Brian Laws (sub)	44 2 1	3	4	3	21 1	60 3 0
1981–82 Third Division 1st 80pts (prom) champions	Alan Stevenson William O'Rourke	46	6	2	4 1	21	60 5
1982–83 Second Division 21st 44pts (rel)	Alan Stevenson William O'Rourke Paul McGee (sub) Brian Laws (sub)	32 10 1 1	5 2	9		7 1	72 15 1 2
1983–84 Third Division 12th 62pts	Roger Hansbury	46	5	2	4	15	77

Season	Goalkeeper	League	FA Cup Apps	FL Cup Apps	Other	Total Clean Sheets	Total Goals Conceded
1984–85 Third Division 21st 46pts (rel)	Roger Hansbury	37	3	4	2	7	77
	Joe Neenan	9			2	3	13
1985–86 Fourth Division 14th 59pts	Joe Neenan	36	2	2	2	8	62
	Dennis Peacock	8				2	16
	Philip Harrington	2				1	1
1986–87 Fourth Division 22nd 49pts	Joe Neenan	45	1	2	3	10	81
	Anthony Woodworth	1					6
1987–88 Fourth Division 10th 67pts	Chris Pearce	46	1	4	8	20	72
1988–89 Fourth Division 16th 55pts	Chris Pearce	39	1	4	3	17	57
	David Williams	7				1	13

Season	Goalkeeper	League	FA Cup Apps	FL Cup Apps	Other	Total Clean Sheets	Total Goals Conceded
1989–90 Fourth Division 16th 56pts	Chris Pearce	39	6	2	2	15	63
	David Williams	7				3	6
1990–91 Fourth Division 6th 79pts	Chris Pearce	43	3	4	5	17	61
	David Williams	3			2	1	10
	Andy Farrell (sub)	1					0
1991–92 Fourth Division 1st 83pts (prom) champions	Chris Pearce	14	4	2	2	5	27
	Nicol Walker	6			1	5	4
	Andrew Marriott	15			4	7	17
	Mark Kendall	2	1			1	7
	David Williams	5					6
1992–93 Second Division 13th 61pts	Marlon Beresford	44	5	2	2	10	70
	David Williams	2				1	7
	Mark Monington (sub)	1					0
1993–94 Second Division 6th 73pts (prom)	Marlon Beresford	46	4	4	5	14	75
1994–95 First Division 22nd 46pts (rel)	Marlon Beresford	40	4	4		4	78
	Wayne Russell	6(2)	1			2	9

Season	Goalkeeper	League	FA Cup Apps	FL Cup Apps	Other	Total Clean Sheets	Total Goals Conceded
1995–96 Second Division 17th 55pts	Marlon Beresford	36	1	4	4	14	67
	Wayne Russell	10				1	16
1996–97 Second Division 9th 68pts	Marlon Beresford	40	4	2	2	14	54
	Wayne Russell	6		2		2	12
1997–98 Second Division 20th 52pts	Marlon Beresford	34	2	4	3	9	63
	Chris Woods	12			2	3	20
1998–99 Second Division 15th 55pts	Paul Chrichton	29			1	7	50
	Gavin Ward	17				2	24
	Anthony Parks						5
	Frank Kval		1	2			3
1999–2000 Second Division 2nd 88pts (prom)	Paul Chrichton	46	4	2	1	21	58
2000–01 First Division 7th 72pts	Paul Chrichton (as sub)	7 1	2	2 2		2	12
	Nikolaos Michopoulos	39				15	52
2001–02 First Division 7th 75pts	Nikolaos Michopoulos	33	2	1		12	51
	Marlon Beresford	13	1			1	15
	Luigi Cennamo (sub)						2

Season	Goalkeeper	League	FA Cup Apps	FL Cup Apps	Other	Total Clean Sheets	Total Goals Conceded
2002–03 First Division 16th 55pts	Nikolaos Michopoulos	13	1			5	19
	Marlon Beresford (as sub)	33 1	5	4		11	78
2003–04 First Division 19th 53pts	Brian Jenson	46	3	3		12	83
2004–05 Champion-ship 13th 60pts	Danny Coyne	20		2		8	21
	Brian Jenson (as sub)	26 1	4	2		14	27
2005–06 Champion-ship 17th 54pts	Danny Coyne (as sub)	7 1		2		2	11
	Brian Jenson (as sub)	38 1	1	1		14	45
	Lee Grant	1				1	0
	John Spicer (sub)	1					2
2006–07 Champion-ship 15th 57pts	Brian Jenson (as sub)	30 1	1	1		13	35
	Danny Coyne	12				2	13
	Mike Pollitt	4				1	5
2007–08 Champion-ship 13th 62pts	Gabor Kiraly	27	1	1		6	38
	Brian Jenson	19		2		5	33

Season	Goalkeeper	League	FA Cup Apps	FL Cup Apps	Other	Total Clean Sheets	Total Goals Conceded
2008–09 Champion-ship 5th 76pts (prom)	Brian Jenson Diego Penny	45 1	5	7	3	21	70 4
2009–10 Premiership 18th 30pts (rel)	Brian Jenson Diego Penny (as sub)	38 1	2	1		3	85 3
2010–11 Champion-ship 8th 68pts	Lee Grant Brian Jenson	25 21	3	3		5 6	44 28
2011–12 Champion-ship 13th 62pts	Lee Grant (as sub) Brian Jenson	42 1 4	1	4		12	64 5
2012–13 Champion-ship 11th 61pts	Lee Grant Brian Jenson (as sub)	46 1	1	1 2		12	61 5
2013–14 Champion-ship 2nd 93pts (prom)	Tom Heaton Alex Cisak (as sub)	46 1	1	3 1		20 1	43 1

Season	Goalkeeper	League	FA Cup Apps	FL Cup Apps	Other	Total Clean Sheets	Total Goals Conceded
2014–15 Premiership 19th 33pts (rel)	Tom Heaton Matt Gilks	38	2	1		10	58 1
2015–16 Champion-ship 1st 93pts (prom)	Tom Heaton Matt Gilks	46	2	1		20	38 1
2016–17 Premier League 16th 40 pts	Tom Heaton Paul Robinson Nick Pope	35 3	1 3	1		10 3	49 7 1

SPECIAL THANKS TO THE FOLLOWING

Steve Caron from JMD Media, Publishing.

John Plunkett for original design.

Ron Brown for his artwork.

Dave Thomas for photographic material.

Elaine East for her typing assistance.

Burnley Football Club for the use of photographic materials.

Carl Sanderson, Burnley FC hospitality officer.

Clarets Mad website.

John Hendley, Press officer of Wolverhampton Wanderers,
for photographic material.

Pauline Scott, former Burnley Football Club secretary.

London Clarets for their support.

The Cystic Fibrosis Trust.

My three children who have supported me.

And a special thanks to the following who have supported me
through good times and bad, who never gave up on this venture:

Keith Franklin.

Pauline Pratley.

Peter Clarke from Malta.

Ex defender Colin Waldron.

And present Burnley goalkeeper Tom Heaton.

ND - #0105 - 270225 - C0 - 234/156/10 - PB - 9781780915395 - Gloss Lamination